THE WORKSHOP FOR MORALITY

THE ISLAMIC CREATIVITY OF PESANTREN DAARUT TAUHID IN BANDUNG, JAVA

THE WORKSHOP FOR MORALITY

THE ISLAMIC CREATIVITY OF PESANTREN DAARUT TAUHID IN BANDUNG, JAVA

Dindin Solahudin

A thesis submitted in partial fulfilment of the degree of Master of Arts in the Department of Archaeology and Anthropology Faculty of Arts The Australian National University February 1996

Published by ANU E Press
The Australian National University
Canberra ACT 0200, Australia
Email: anuepress@anu.edu.au
This title available online at: http://epress.anu.edu.au/morality_citation.html

---

National Library of Australia
Cataloguing-in-Publication entry

Author: Solahudin, Dindin.

Title: The workshop for morality : the islamic creativity of Pesantren Daarat Tauhid in Bandung, Java / author,

             Dindin Solahudin

Publisher: Acton, A.C.T. : ANU E Press, 2008.

ISBN: 9781921313677 (pbk.) 9781921313684 (pdf)

Notes: Bibliography.

Subjects: Pesantren Daarut Tauhid (Bandung, Indonesia)
             Islamic education--Indonesia--Bandung.
             Islamic religious education--Indonesia--Bandung.
             Community leadership--Indonesia--Bandung.
             Islam and state--Indonesia--Bandung.
             Islam--Indonesia--Bandung--Social life and customs.

Dewey Number: 297.7795982

All rights reserved. No part of this publication may be reproduced, stored in a retrieval system or transmitted in any form or by any means, electronic, mechanical, photocopying or otherwise, without the prior permission of the publisher.

Cover design by ANU E Press

This edition © 2008 ANU E Press

Islam in Southeast Asia Series

Theses at The Australian National University are assessed by external examiners and students are expected to take into account the advice of their examiners before they submit to the University Library the final versions of their theses. For this series, this final version of the thesis has been used as the basis for publication, taking into account other changes that the author may have decided to undertake. In some cases, a few minor editorial revisions have made to the work. The acknowledgements in each of these publications provide information on the supervisors of the thesis and those who contributed to its development. For many of the authors in this series, English is a second language and their texts reflect an appropriate fluency.

Table of Contents

Foreword	ix
Acknowledgments	xi
Notes on Foreign Language	xiii
Abstract	xv
1. Introduction	1
1.1 The Study in Perspective	1
1.2 The Pesantren Tradition	3
1.3 Daarut Tauhid: A Pesantren Milieu	6
1.4 The Organisation of the Work	9
2. Initial Stages and Foundation	13
2.1 The Founder: K. H. Abdullah Gymnastiar	13
2.2 *I'tikaf* and *Lailatul Qodar*	17
2.3 The Dreams Involving the Prophet Muhammad	21
2.4 The *Hajj* and The *Umrah*	26
2.5 The *Shilaturrahmi*	31
2.6 The Foundation of Daarut Tauhid	35
3. The Leader, the Followers, and the Pattern of Relationships	41
3.1 The Leader: Personal Qualities and Popularity	41
3.2 *Ma'unah*: the Miraculous Power of Aa Gym	46
3.3 The Followers: Numbers, Diversity, and Identity	47
3.4 The Followers: Reasons for Joining	50
3.5 The Patterns of Relationship	55
4. Creative Expression Eschatological and Worldly Orientations	61
4.1 The World and Beyond: A Balance	61
4.2 Inner Dynamics: A Harmonious Combination	67
4.3 Modesty and Modernity: A Wonderful Combination	70
4.4 Multi-style Management: A Solid Combination	72
5. Daarut Tauhid as the *Bengkel Akhlaq* Religion and Morality	77
5.1 Moral Decadence	78
5.2 *Qolbun Salim*: Qualities of Heart and Mind	81
5.3 *Taushiyah Penyejuk Hati*	85
5.4 Ritual Weeping: Nature and Structure	91
5.5 Ritual Weeping: Meaning and Function	98

6. Conclusion 103
Selected Glossary 107
Bibliography 115

Foreword

This volume, *The Workshop for Morality* by Dindin Solahudin is a remarkable study of a most unusual pesantren. Officially known as Pesantren Daarut Tauhid, this pesantren was located in Bandung and flourished at the beginning of a period of Islamic resurgence in Indonesia. More commonly referred to as the *Bengkel Akhlaq*, this 'Workshop for Morality' exerted a special appeal to groups of young urban Muslims, particularly students. Its founder was H. K. Abdullah Gymnastiar, popularly known as Aa Gym, who later went on to become one of Indonesia's most important Muslim preachers and television celebrities.

Pesantren Daarut Tauhid was notable for the popularity of Aa Gym's preaching and the emotional response that he affected among his followers. Ritual weeping was a prominent feature of gatherings at the pesantren. But Pesantren Daarut Tauhid was also unusual for the way that it organized the teaching of classic Islamic texts (*kitab klassik*) by inviting distinguished religious teachers from other West Javanese pesantren to lecture at different times during the week and to present varying Islamic orientations.

Dindin Solahudin did his fieldwork for this study in the mid-1990s and is able to provide exceptional insights into the operations of Pesantren Daarut Tauhid while at the same time conveying a sense of the religious enthusiasm that characterized this period. He was also able to speak, at some length, with its founder, Aa Gym, and on this basis, he presents a picture of Aa Gym's early life and of the initial setbacks and subsequent spiritual experiences that were to transform his life. He highlights the importance of dreams and the profound experience of the *hajj* that prompted the first stirring of his preaching career and the eventual establishment of his pesantren.

As particularly pertinent to an understanding of Pesantren Daarut Tauhid's mission as a 'Workshop for Morality', Dindin Solahudin examines Aa Gym's formulation of the qualities of mind and heart that he sees as fundamental to an Islamic morality: sincerity, modesty, honesty and patience. The attainment of these qualities was the purpose of all religious activities of the pesantren.

The Workshop for Morality is a superb work of both historical and ethnographic relevance that reflects the capacity of its author, Dindin Solahudin, to capture a critical moment in the development of Islam in contemporary Indonesian society. A native of Bandung, Dindin Solahudin has had an association since 1993 with the former State Institute for Islamic Studies (IAIN) Sunan Gunung Jati that has now become a State Islamic University in Bandung. On the Faculty of Dakwah and Communication, he has, at different times, headed both the Department of Journalism and the Department of Community Development. Since 1996, he has also been a lecturer at Pesantren Al-Ihsan. Since his graduation from The Australian National University in 1998, he has continued to do research and to publish on a wide range of topics. He is currently engaged in the study of Islamic moderation for a doctoral degree at the State Islamic University Sunan Kalijaga in Yogyakarta

James J. Fox

Acknowledgments

First of all, I am immeasurably indebted to Professor James J. Fox, my principal supervisor, who invited me to study Anthropology at the Australian National University. His generous guidance and continuous encouragement have extended my understanding of the Anthropology of Islam. He has been particularly instrumental in the period of my thesis writing not only in offering insightful criticisms and suggestions, but also in tirelessly correcting errors in my English expression. I am grateful to Dr. Patrick Guinness, my co-supervisor, whose questions and comments have been very stimulating. My gratitude also goes to Dr. M. Lyon, my adviser, for her advice. I, however, accept full responsibility for the academic content of this work.

A major debt is also owed to my sponsor *AusAid* (Australian Agency for International Development) which enabled me to take advantage of this very valuable opportunity to study in Australia. Members of the staff at *AusAid*, in both Jakarta and Canberra, deserve my deepest thanks for their generous financial, material and spiritual support and assistance.

I am grateful to Dr. Nicolas Peterson who guided me in my course work right from my first arrival. My gratitude also goes to Prof. Francesca Merlan and all the staff of the Department of Archaeology and Anthropology, Faculty of Arts, and the Department of Anthropology, Research School of Pacific Studies, for their remarkable help over the two years of my study at the Australian National University. My special thank-you goes to all my friends at the ANU who have given me help and support throughout my study. They were particularly helpful when they asked me 'how is your thesis going?'

The people of Daarut Tauhid, and in Bandung at large, deserve my sincere expression of thanks. I owe a particular debt of gratitude to Aa Gym, the *kyai* of Daarut Tauhid, who willingly devoted so much time to talk with me, in the midst of his extra-busy preaching schedule. All the officials at Daarut Tauhid were very helpful to me in carrying out my research. The *santri* and *jamaah* of Daarut Tauhid were also very open and sincere in sharing their views and feelings. They are too many to mention all of them here, but each is a precious memory. I am grateful to them all and I can only say *hatur nuhun*.

Last, but not least, I express my loving acknowledgment and heartfelt gratitude to Rida, my wife, and Tiaz, my son, to whom this work is dedicated. They shared with me all the emotional dynamics of my study. We were apart during the first year of my study: I was in Canberra while Rida and Tiaz were in Indonesia. I could not even witness the birth of my son and only saw him for the first time when he was six months old. During the second year, accompanying me in Canberra, they patiently and understandingly tolerated my absence from their company, often over night. I also deeply thankful to my wife Rida for her assistance in I transcribing a huge stack of fieldwork tape recordings.

Notes on Foreign Language

I have tried to incorporate in this work a number of vernacular terms commonly used in Pesantren Daarut Tauhid. These include Arabic, Sundanese, Javanese, and Indonesian terms. These languages are important in understanding the cultural context of the research. This is particularly crucial where there is no precise equivalent in English. For example, the word *shalat* and *do'a*, two different concepts, are usually equally translated as 'prayer.' Confusion may arise if I simply say 'prayer,' since it can mean either *shalat* or *do'a*. Some writers, such as J. R. Bowen, has solved this problem by translating *shalat* as 'worship.' However, 'worship' may also mean *ibadah*, which is much wider in meaning than *shalat*. To avoid this confusion, these vernacular terms appear as such throughout this work. I have provided the English translation of the words in their first appearance.

Arabic, Indonesian, Sundanese, and Javanese words appearing in this work have the same form for singular and plural. I have not anglicised these words by adding an 's' to denote the plural. Words such as *shalat, kyai, santri*, and *pesantren*, for example, may represent either singular or plural forms.

English translations of verses of the Qur'an quoted in this work follow *The Qur'an; English Translation of "The Meanings and Commentary"* issued by the Kingdom of Saudi Arabia (1993), Medina: King Fahd Complex for the Printing of the Holy Qur'an.

Abstract

This ethnographic study attempts to portray Pesantren Daarut Tauhid in Bandung, Java, in terms of its emergence, its nature and structure, and the role it plays in the reinforcement of Islamic morality in a Muslim community. The initial stages and the foundation of the pesantren are first discussed in order to understand a number of events which were crucial to the emergence of the pesantren. The work then examines the nature of the leader and his followers and the structure of interrelationships between them. Next, the practice of Islam at the pesantren is discussed in order to consider its creativity in expressing Islam. Finally, the work discusses the ways by which the pesantren reinforces religious morality.

The study shows that the establishment of the pesantren was related in some ways to the general phenomenon of Islamic resurgence. However, it does not follow the common notion that Islamic resurgence involves the internal reformation of Islamic practices in response to the local influences of religious practices. It is, instead, more a response to the social problems and ills that are a reflection of the erosion of religious life. Unlike the reformist Muhammadiyah and PERSIS, Daarut Tauhid attempts less to purge Islamic teachings and practices of non-Islamic influences than to call Muslims to a disciplined practice of Islam, regardless of which lines of Islam they follow. In the light of this, Daarut Tauhid focuses its attention on the earnest application of Islamic morality. By choosing this aspect, the pesantren is less likely to be trapped in the endless religious dispute between modernist and traditionalist because the two groups have no disagreement in this respect.

The study also shows that Pesantren Daarut Tauhid, unlike other pesantren, plays a deliberate, direct role in the reinforcement of Islamic morality. First, it is known as the pesantren *Bengkel Akhlaq* (Workshop for Morality), an institution where Muslims can rehabilitate their immoral behaviour. Secondly, daily life is redeveloped to foster Islamic morality in order to refine Muslims' morality. In this sphere, the relationship between the leader and the follower is both collective and personal. Thirdly, *akhlaq* (Islamic morality) is always the central theme of all public talks and written publications. Fourthly, spiritual workshops are regularly conducted in order to provide a forum where Muslims can rehabilitate their morality. Here, the tradition of spiritual weeping is effectively used to generate religious consciousness and, in turn, to propagate virtue.

Pesantren Daarut Tauhid has made a considerable contribution to the pesantren tradition in Java. Geographically, it extends the influence of the pesantren tradition in an urban area whereas most pesantren are concentrated in rural areas. Functionally, it enriches the pesantren tradition as a centre for quick and effective moral rehabilitation. While pesantren conventionally focus on learning advanced Islamic knowledge, Daarut Tauhid turns to the more practical knowledge of conduct. The existence of Pesantren Daarut Tauhid, with these two distinctive features, can be seen as complementary to the existing pesantren tradition at large, in that it does not belittle rural and conventional traditions of pesantren, but it empowers them by widening their influence to the urban area and enriching their styles.

Chapter 1: Introduction

This is a study of Pesantren[1] Daarut Tauhid in Bandung, Java, focusing on its role in the reinforcement of Islamic morality in a contemporary community of Muslims. As a pesantren, Daarut Tauhid is part of the pesantren tradition in Java and thus shares similar features with other pesantren. Yet as a newly emergent institution, it bears novel characteristics that reflect the influence of both local tradition and contemporary modern civilisation.

In a wider perspective, the rise of Pesantren Daarut Tauhid can be understood as part of the worldwide phenomena of Islamic resurgence. In this case, Daarut Tauhid demonstrates the dynamics of Islam and the flexibility these demand. Hence I argue that in undergoing resurgence, Islam accommodates both local and global cultures without necessarily losing its definition.[2]

In a more specific context, Pesantren Daarut Tauhid is part of the pesantren tradition in Indonesia.[3] The relationship of Daarut Tauhid to the pesantren tradition at large is just like its relationship to Islamic resurgence; it shows the dynamics and the subsequent flexibility of the pesantren tradition. Thus, I argue that Daarut Tauhid has enriched the diversity of the pesantren tradition.[4] The most fundamental contribution Daarut Tauhid makes is its efficacy in the reinforcement of Islamic morality among urban Muslims.[5]

1.1 The Study in Perspective

Professor Clifford Geertz concludes, in his latest work, *After the Fact* (1995:165), that "what is happening both in those places [Sefrou in Morocco and Pare in Indonesia] and elsewhere to "Islam" [original quote]...is losing definition and gaining energy." This suggests that Islam, in Indonesia and elsewhere, is now in revival but, to achieve this, it has to lose its definition. This judgment of Geertz's is based on his observation that

> secularism, commodification, corruption, selfishness, immorality, rootlessness, general estrangement from the sources of value, all the ills attributed to the modern form of life as it has taken shape in the West (and especially, everyone's hard case, in the United States), loom, or seem to, as imminent threats, and the risk of havoc looks at least as real as the promise of ease (1995:142-143).

My question, in response to this Geertzian conclusion, is which definition of Islam does Geertz observe Islam to be losing? Geertz seems to uphold his narrow cultural definition of Islam which has been much criticised from as early as his first masterpiece, *The Religion of Java* (1960). That is his narrow definition of Islam which excludes so many Islamic features from Islam. Marshall Hodgson, the most fundamental critic of Geertz's view in this regard, criticises Geertz for "labelling much of the Muslim religious life in Java 'Hindu'…[and for identifying] a long series of phenomena, virtually universal to Islam and sometimes found even in the Qur'an itself, as un-Islamic" (1974:551n). The narrowness of Geertz's definition of Islam was put clearly by Nakamura who shows how Geertz reduces Islam. According to Nakamura (1984:72), what Geertz conceives of as the core values of Javanese tradition, i.e. *sabar, iklas*, and *slamet*, are all Islamic in origin and are understood by Javanese people as they are in their original Islamic meanings.[6] Regarding these values as un-Islamic thus means reducing Islam.

Moreover, since those values are rooted in the Qur'an, they are also, in fact, commonly applied among modernist Muslims. Hence, Geertz's definition of Islam is, to me, even narrower than that which is perceived by the modernist line of Islamic thought. Therefore, I see the weakness of this Geertzian definition to be more than what Hodgson and Nakamura accuse him of as having the modernist bias. It is, instead, a categorical bias. By this I mean that Geertz, in categorising Javanese Muslims into his trichotomy, *santri-abangan-priyayi*,[7] excludes some traditions from Islam in order to include them in the less or non-Islamic traditions of *abangan* and *priyayi*. As Nakamura (1984:72) has shown, the *abangan* core ritual, *slametan*, and the *priyayi* core values, as mentioned above, are Islamic in origin. And Hodgson (1974:551n) considers that Geertz's comprehensive data in *The Religion of Java* demonstrate the complete triumph of Islam in Java, so that very little from the Hindu past has survived even in inner Java.

It is however misleading to assume that the Hindu past and local beliefs have completely disappeared from Java. Surely, animism, deism, and overall spirit beliefs do still persist in Java. Geertz would have been right if he had elaborated these kinds of local beliefs when discussing the Javanese outlook (Koentjaraningrat 1963:191). But with the coming of Islam to Java those beliefs have mixed considerably, influencing each other. While Hodgson finds these local beliefs have been Islamised, Geertz, on the contrary, finds Islam has been localised. Geertz thus argues that Muslim religious life in Java looks more Javanese than Middle-Eastern (1976:367–368). And now, after four decades, Geertz goes further to argue that not only has Islam been Javanised but it has lost its definition, so much so that he puts the intactness of Islam in doubt by way of putting the term between quotes (1995:165).

As a matter of fact, Islam as a world religion has been and will always be in dialogue with both local and global cultures. In the light of this assumption, what is happening to Islam may not be seen as a Geertzian loss of definition but can be better understood as the inherent flexibility of Islam, a necessary feature for its cultural dialogue.[8] This is in accordance with the Muslims' belief that Islam is a universal religion. Universality requires a great deal of flexibility in regard to local cultures. While Geertz, in observing Balinese religion, was quite right in viewing this kind of religious flexibility as the dynamics of religion (1979), he failed to see the vigorous development of Islam today, in Java and elsewhere, as an example of this dynamism.

The dynamics of Islam has been recognised throughout the world particularly by its inclination for resurgence.[9] By this resurgence, following Muzaffar (1987:2), I mean any attempt to reinforce Islamic morality entirely in its personal and social practices. This resurgence is not necessarily political in nature.[10] It can be and often is a flexible and capable creativity of the Muslim community to adopt and adapt both global modernity, with its inherent technology, and local cultures.

Pesantren Daarut Tauhid, with which this study deals, may be a good example of a Muslim community of this kind. It flexibly adopts and adapts the current inclination of world civilisation. At the same time, it genuinely incorporates local cultures. It has thus successfully avoided any conflict between the two realms and in so doing, it has not departed from Islam.[11]

1.2 The Pesantren Tradition

Zamakhsyari Dhofier, with his *The Pesantren Tradition: A Study of the Role of the Kyai in the Maintenance of the Traditional Ideology of Islam in Java* (1980), was the first to provide a comprehensive study of the pesantren tradition in Java and Madura. The translation and publication of Dhofier's study in Indonesian has made wide-spread the understanding of the pesantren world (Zulkifli 1994:3). Before this little was known among scholars about the pesantren institutions, which are "the lynch pins of Islamization" in South East Asia (Johns 1975:40).

Notwithstanding the fact that studies of the pesantren can be traced back to the second half of the nineteenth century when Brumund studied the educational system in Java in 1857, these studies were viewed to be partial. Dhofier (1980a: 1-3) thus evaluates that

> scholars such as van den Berg, Hurgronje and Geertz...have only partially understood features of pesantren life. Their descriptions of pesantren life have only touched upon the simplicity of the buildings within pesantren complexes, the austerity of the *santri* way of life, the *santri* absolute obedience to their *kyai* and, in some instances, on the preliminary teaching of some Arabic texts. Even Raden Achmad Djajadiningrat...revealed more about the inconvenience of pesantren life than of the real strength of pesantren tradition.

In the poverty of this academic record, the origins of the pesantren institutions in Java have been a matter of controversy. Dhofier (1984:20) speculates that the pesantren tradition originated from simple gatherings for learning Islam, which began to emerge in the fifteenth century. This seems too early to van Bruinessen (1992:76–77), who believes that the earliest pesantren to be Pesantren Tegalsari, in East Java, which was established in 1742. To van Bruinessen, what existed before this century were only Islamic gatherings in mosques, holy graves, and palaces, which could not yet be called pesantren (ibid). An earlier speculative date has been put forward by the Department of Religious Affairs, which suggests that Pesantren Jan Tampes II, in Pamekasan, Madura, established in 1062, is the oldest pesantren ever founded (Mastuhu 1994:19). This is of course questionable, as Mastuhu notes, for there had to be a Pesantren Jan Tampes I, which must be older than Pesantren Jan Tampes II.

The difference between van Bruinessen and Dhofier lies in how they regard those earliest gatherings for learning Islam. Whereas the former regards them as not yet proper pesantren, the latter sees them as the embryo of pesantren institutions. Thus, to Dhofier, those gatherings, referred to as the *pengajian*,[12] were a necessary part of the pesantren tradition (1980a:27–29). Dhofier's view explains why Abdurrahman Wahid (1984:7), the leader of Nahdhatul Ulama,[13] claims that the pesantren tradition began to emerge as early as the coming of Islam to Indonesia in the thirteenth century. Wahid's claim is confirmed by Abubakar Atjeh (1957:43), who regards Shaikh Mawlana Malik Ibrahim, one of *Wali Sanga* (the nine saints) who is believed to be one of the bringers of Islam to Java (Fox 1991, Geertz 1976:39), as the founder of the first pesantren. Hence, unlike van Bruinessen, Atjeh seems to be certain that the term 'pesantren' had existed as early as the thirteenth century.[14]

In fact, these views can be combined despite their apparent contradiction. We may imagine from these views that the pesantren tradition was much simpler in its early development than it is today. This simplicity of the earliest form of pesantren is suggested, for example, by Nurcholis Madjid and Zulkifli (1994:3). Madjid (1988:104) speculates that the pesantren tradition, as an educational institution, originated from spots where followers of Sufi orders stopped and performed some rituals.[15] As Islamic instructions were taught at those spots, these "stations" ended up being centres for learning Islam, which Dhofier might refer to as *pengajian*.

My present study of Pesantren Daarut Tauhid may help to clarify these speculations about the origins of the pesantren tradition. As we shall see, Daarut Tauhid grew out of a small group of *pengajian*. While it was officially founded as a pesantren in 1990, in its pioneering form of *pengajian* it began three years earlier in 1987. The process through which Daarut Tauhid has progressed may reflect the natural process of the outgrowth of the pesantren tradition in its earliest existence. That is, the pesantren tradition might have begun as a simple locus for learning Islam and, as time passed, it grew further to be known as pesantren.[16]

Much has been written regarding variety and complexity in the pesantren tradition through time (Dhofier 1980a:46; Mastuhu 1994; Tebba 1985:269; Zulkifli 1994:3-4). Dhofier (1980a:46) recognises two general types of pesantren: *salafi* and *khalafi*. The former preserves "the teaching of classical texts as essential education...without the introduction of secular subjects." The latter either introduces secular subjects or incorporates secular schools in addition to the study of classical texts. Mastuhu (1994:19) discusses some of the specialisation by which pesantren are distinguished. For example, Pesantren Blok Agung, at Banyuwangi, East Java, is known for its specialisation in studying Al-Ghazali's *tasauf*; Pesantren Tebuireng, East Java, is known as a pesantren for Hadith and Fiqh (Islamic Jurisprudence); and Pesantren Guluk-guluk, on Madura, is known as a pesantren for *dakwah bil hal* (practical proselytization). In short, each pesantren has come to have its own "trademark" in spite of its coverage of all branches of Islamic studies.[17]

In Bandung, one can find many pesantren well-known for their own specialisation. Pesantren Babussalam in Dago, Northern Bandung, is well-known as a pesantren al-Qur'an, specialising on the study of *tafsir* (commentary). Pesantren Al-Falah in Cicalengka, Eastern Bandung, is also famous as a pesantren Al-Qur'an, but specialising on *qiroat*, that is, various styles of reciting Qur'an including ethics and melody.[18] Pesantren Al-Jawamy in Cileunyi, Eastern Bandung, while is known as an all-inclusive pesantren, is still better known for its monopoly of mastering *ilmu falaq*, the Islamic astronomy which is used particularly to determine the lunar calendar of Islam (*hijriyya*) and the prayer (*shalat*) timetable. Pesantren Daarut Tauhid, with which we are dealing, is well-known as the *Bengkel Akhlaq* (the Workshop for Morality).

There are many other pesantren in Bandung, such as Pesantren Sukamiskin in Ujungberung, Pesantren Daarul Arqom in Pacet, Pesantren Al-Basyariyah in Cibaduyut, Pesantren At-Taqwa in Cimindi, Cimahi, Pesantren Cijerah and so on. The pesantren tradition in Bandung is as prominently well-rooted as in other parts of West Java. This partly explains why Glicken (1987:240) states that "West Java, as a whole, is the most strongly Islamic province on the island of Java and, indeed, one of the strongest Islamic areas in Indonesia." However, should one refer to Dhofier's map of pesantren centres in Java (1980a:x^a, 1982:3), one will be left with the impression that there would be no pesantren at all in Bandung, since there, on the map, is no mark of any pesantren in Bandung. However, Dhofier acknowledged (1980a:5) that he confined his study of the pesantren tradition to Central and East Java, thus excluding West Java, whose capital city is Bandung.[19]

This work attempts to provide a first step in filling this gap. Based on fieldwork carried out between December 1994 and February 1995 on Pesantren Daarut Tauhid in Bandung, it attempts to provide a brief ethnographic report on this pesantren, focusing on its role as a moral force among Muslims in Bandung. While this study confirms some points of previous studies, it attempts to expand on some points of previous works on Islam, in general, and on the pesantren tradition, in particular.

1.3 Daarut Tauhid: A Pesantren Milieu

Pesantren Daarut Tauhid is located in Gegerkalong, the northern part of the city of Bandung. Gegerkalong is only about four kilometres away from the *alun-alun* (square, the heart of Bandung city) and just about two kilometres from *pendopo gubernur* (the offices of the provincial governor). It is in the same *kelurahan* (suburb) with IKIP Bandung (*Institut Keguruan Ilmu Pendidikan Bandung*, Bandung Public Institute for Educational Studies) and is in neighbourhood to such national universities as ITB (*Institut Teknologi Bandung*, Bandung Institute of Technology), Unpad (*Universitas Padjadjaran*, Padjadjaran University),[20] and Unisba (*Universitas Islam Bandung*, Bandung University of Islamic Studies).

Known as the Pesantren *Bengkel Akhlaq*, Daarut Tauhid is a pesantren both because it formally declares itself as a pesantren and because it meets the basic criteria of a pesantren. It meets the minimum elements of a pesantren, monumentally set forth by Zamakhsyari Dhofier (1982:49–59). Those basic elements are the *pondok* (dormitories), the mosque, the study of classical Islamic *kitab* (texts), the *santri* (students), and the *kyai* (leader).

The element *pondok* of Pesantren Daarut Tauhid takes the form of permanent buildings divided into rooms each variably inhabited by five to ten santri. These may be owned by the pesantren or be privately owned and in the vicinity of the pesantren. There is, so far, only one Daarut Tauhid owned *pondok* which has six bedrooms. This dormitory is now inhabited by female santri. Other dormitories, that are occupied by male santri, are not owned by the pesantren. They are, instead, houses rented and thus paid for by Daarut Tauhid whilst the inhabitant santri share the payment. This rental phenomenon is not so startling for at least three reasons. First, as shall be elaborated in chapter three, most santri are school or university students who come from a distance and thus are used to living in rented rooms. When intending to study in Daarut Tauhid, they simply move in and rent a room already booked by Daarut Tauhid. This is supported by the second reason, that is, the urban location of Daarut Tauhid. As noted by Dhofier (1980a:47), the rental tradition is a common phenomenon among the students of Islamic study-centres in cities such as Mecca and Madina. The third reason is the fact that Daarut Tauhid is still in its early development. It just built its big mosque in 1992, female dormitory and mini-market in 1993, mini-bank and mini-restaurant in early 1994, and a study building in late 1994. So it is simply a matter of time and priority, while the building of other facilities has been given priority over the building of more dormitories.

What is startling is the fact that the *kyai*'s house itself is still a rented one. It is in a sense part of the *pondok* because part of the house is inhabited by some santri. Unlike the rest of the *pondok*, however, this house is not paid for by the pesantren but by the *kyai* himself. As a matter of fact, the *kyai* had had his own house, certainly bought by his own money, yet it was given as the site for the new mosque as his sincere *waqf* (donation for religious use).

The capacity of all *pondok* together, apart from the mosque and the study spaces, is enough for no more than about a hundred santri. There are two reasons for this limited *pondok* facilities. First, Daarut Tauhid was officially founded only in 1990; this, together with the present rental conditions, reflects the early stage of the development of this pesantren. Second, at least up until now, most of the followers did not stay in the pesantren but attended the pesantren's activities without necessarily staying in the pesantren complex.[21]

Photograph 1 Daarut Tauhid mosque as the centre of activities. Pedicab, car, and the busy street in front of the mosque suggest the urban location of the mosque

The *pondok* involves the separation of the sexes as is common to all pesantren in Indonesia. Male santri have their own *pondok* as do female santri. So also do they have their own "office" and managing authorities. As in other pesantren (Dhofier 1980a:48), these two sex-based "realms" are well-separated by the *kyai*'s house. The female *pondok* is far better off than the male *pondok* in terms of both the physical construction of the building and its supporting facilities. Bathrooms for females, for example, are built-in at their *pondok* unlike those for males. Among the reasons given for this privilege for female santri is the assumption that women are viewed weaker than men, and the *kyai*'s effort to observe Islamic law such that unnecessary, and perhaps dangerous, intercourse between Muslims of different sexes is to be avoided. One of the ways of keeping women separated from men is to provide women with special, often inevitably better, facilities.

The *masjid* (mosque) serves as the second element of Pesantren Daarut Tauhid. It was built in 1992 on the land that was formerly the private property of the *kyai* and thus has replaced his former house.[22] It is a two storey building with the capacity for about 1000 praying or 2000 sitting Muslims. Located at the centre of the pesantren area, it is, indeed, the centre of pesantren activities.

The third element for the pesantren, the study of classical texts (*kitab-kitab klasik*), is also identifiable in Pesantren Daarut Tauhid. The *kyai*, when delivering his weekly *pengajian* (public sermon) on Thursdays, refers to and explores the meaning of a certain *kitab klasik*, concerned with the Islamic guidance of morality. Daarut Tauhid has, as well, a scheduled program for the study of Islamic classical texts. This is done on Mondays, Tuesdays, and Wednesdays evening.

An unusual feature here is the presence of outsider *kyai* other than the Daarut Tauhid's *kyai*. While other pesantren are self-sufficient with their own *kyai* or *ustadz* (young teacher), Daarut Tauhid invites *kyai* from other pesantren to teach there. For example, at Monday sessions, Daarut Tauhid invites K. H. Drs. Jalaluddin Asy-Syatibi, the *kyai* of Pesantren Miftahul Khoir, Dago. At Tuesday sessions, it invites K. H. Irfan Qusyairi, the *kyai* of Pesantren At-Taqwa, Cimindi. They are, in a sense, *kyai tamu* (guest instructors) with a different background of knowledge and different orientations to the various religious schools of thought (*madzhab*). There is thus direct encounter between different *madzhab*, which has produced endless contention in Indonesia, since each *mazhab* has its own advocates.[23] According to one of the officials at the pesantren, this tradition is being developed to create a friendly sphere of intercourse between varying lines of Islamic thoughts, in the spirit of *shilaturrahmi* (bonds of friendship). Daarut Tauhid itself is therefore known for promoting a new orientation; *madzhab shilaturrahmi*, with the spirit of conflict avoidance.

The fourth element of Pesantren Daarut Tauhid are the *santri*. As already noted, the great majority of Daarut Tauhid's followers do not stay in the complex of the pesantren but come there at certain times for certain activities such as to listen to a public talk, to attend an intensive study of *kitab klasik*, or to carry out short-term workshops.[24]

The final element, the *kyai*, bears many distinctive features that enrich the pesantren tradition. He is a very young *kyai* who, unlike other *kyai*, did not experience pesantren education in a conventional way. If anything, he just visited *kyai* in various pesantren. As Dhofier (1980a) and Pranowo (1991a) record, normally it has been one of the pesantren traditions that a person spend several years in a number of pesantren before he qualifies to be a *kyai*. There are many other distinctive features about this *kyai* of Daarut Tauhid, which are discussed in the two chapters to follow.

1.4 The Organisation of the Work

This work is organised into six chapters including introduction and conclusion. Chapter One, the introduction, provides the necessary background for the study. It attempts first to put the study in the wider perspective of studying Islam, discussing some views on the development of Islam. It then discusses the pesantren tradition of which Daarut Tauhid is a part and to which it contributes. Finally, it presents a portrait of Daarut Tauhid as a pesantren milieu in order to provide a preliminary sketch.

Chapter Two examines the process of the emergence of Pesantren Daarut Tauhid. Events that served as initial stages in the founding and which were very crucial to the birth of the pesantren are analysed here. However, prior to this section, I take up the life of the leader since his childhood as this is necessary background because those events were inseparably linked to the development of his beliefs and therefore his actions. The chapter ends with an account of the process of the official foundation of the pesantren and notes the principal purposes of the foundation. I argue here that the process through which Daarut Tauhid emerged may provide an example of the origins of the pesantren tradition in Java. While archival records on the earliest form of pesantren are poor, it seems likely that it grew out of the *pengajian* tradition in mosques, houses, and other places.

Chapter Three provides a deeper examination of the pesantren's leader, Aa Gym, and an analytical description of his followers, in order to understand the pattern of relationships between the leader, his followers, and the pesantren itself. Here, the personal qualities and popularity of Aa Gym as a *kyai* are discussed. The spiritual power of Aa Gym, as an important element of his leadership, is discussed here as well. Then follows a discussion on the followers: firstly, their numbers, diversity, and identity, and, secondly, their reasons for joining the pesantren.

I describe in Chapter Four the practice of Islam at Pesantren Daarut Tauhid. It is important to understand how members practise Islam, a practice that is in accord with the cultural demands of global and local cultures. This chapter shows that Islam is creatively practised by Muslims at Daarut Tauhid. This creativity manifests itself in the way they combine eschatological and worldly orientations to life.

Chapter Five deals with the very core of Daarut Tauhid's existence, that is, its representation as the *Bengkel Akhlaq* (Workshop for Morality). This chapter includes, first, what is meant by moral decadence. Then, it discusses the concept of *qolbun salim* (sound heart) which is believed by people at Daarut Tauhid to be the solution to moral decadence. Next, this chapter describes the core ritual of the pesantren, that is, what is called *Taushiyah Penyejuk Hati* (Comforting Religious Advice). The indispensability and efficacy of this ritual in comforting the followers are depicted in this chapter. Finally, this chapter considers the ritual weeping that is prominent at Daarut Tauhid. The analysis is focused on the nature and structure and then on the meaning and function of this tradition of ritual weeping.

Finally, Chapter Six provides the concluding remarks of the work and some reflections on the pesantren tradition and Islam at large.

ENDNOTES

[1] Pesantren are generally known as Islamic training centres for advanced studies and, more specifically, as traditional Islamic educational institutions in Java (Dhofier 1980a:viii). However, as my present study will show, its use here means a religious and socio-cultural institution, which thus embraces more functions than mere education.

[2] Thus Tebba (1985:268) assumes that the extraordinary survival of the pesantren tradition over centuries is a result of its ability to respond to every new reality of community development in Indonesia.

[3] The pesantren tradition has cultural features that are not found in other parts of the Muslim world save in Indonesia (Tebba 1985:269).

[4] In consequence, this also denies the assumption that the pesantren tradition is in a state of decay, due to the changing preference of Muslims today to choose secular educational institutions.

[5] Nearly all pesantren are located in rural areas of Indonesia. The pesantren's moral force is thus more felt in these areas than in urban areas.

[6] In fact, as Nakamura has pointed out (1984:72), the terms *sabar, iklas,* and *slamet* can be easily found in the Qur'an. The term *iklas*, for example, is even the title of Chapter 112 of the Qur'an. This term appears frequently in other chapters such as 2:139, 4:146, and 10:23.

[7] It is widely known that Geertz (1960) introduced *abangan, santri,* and *priyayi* as three variants of various Muslim traditions in Java. The *abangan* variant, dominant in the villages, is conceived to hold spirit beliefs and to practise curing, sorcery, and magic, with the *slametan* ritual feast as its core (1976:5). [The *abangan* people are even considered by Alice Dewey (1962:33), Geertz's fellow researcher, as non-Muslims.] The *santri* variant, predominant at markets, is marked by "a careful and regular execution of the basic rituals of Islam...[and] a whole complex of social, charitable, and political Islamic organisations." The *priyayi* variant stresses Hindu aspects and is related to the bureaucratic element (1976:6). This Geertzian categorisation has drawn much criticism. Bachtiar (1985), Hodgson (1974), Koentjaraningrat (1963, 1984), Muchtarom (1988), Nakamura (1984), Pranowo (1991), Suparlan (1976), and Woodward (1989) are among the fundamental critics. Yet, Geertz's fame, particularly as an anthropologist, is said to owe much to the flood of criticisms addressed to him. Like Marx, Geertz's popularity began only after massive criticism of his work (Jamhari 1994:14)

[8] See Kurshid Ahmad (1983:226) for an example of the flexibility of Islam.

[9] For the study of Islamic resurgence in the past two decades, see *Voices of Resurgent Islam*, edited by J. L. Esposito (1983).

[10] I am aware that Islamic resurgence seems most generally to be political. Dessouki (1982:4) thus sees it as the increasing prominence and politicization of Islamic ideologies and symbols.

[11] On a seminar on this pesantren on 12 October 1995, Professor J. J. Fox judged that none of Daarut Tauhid's features departs from Islam.

[12] This kind of traditional education is known in most of the Muslim world as mosque education (Dhofier 1980a:51, 53, 57). Among the Sundanese people of West Java, it is more commonly known as *ngaji*, omitting the prefix *pe* and the suffix *an* from the Indonesian *pengajian*. See Glicken (1987:241, 244) for this tradition of *ngaji* among the Sundanese people.

[13] Nahdhatul Ulama (NU, lit. the Rise of the Religious Scholars) is a conservative Islamic organisation in Indonesia. This socio-religious organisation originated from the pesantren, in that it was found both at pesantren and by pesantren figures, among whom K.H. Hasyim Asy'ary from Pesantren Tebuireng (Dhofier 1980a:141;1982:97,101n). Many pesantren are thus affiliated with NU and the pesantren tradition is most often associated with this organisation (Tebba 1985:276–277).

[14] There is another speculation proposed by I. J. Brugman and K. Meys. Considering the general features of pesantren, they speculate that pesantren-like institutions had existed long before the coming of Islam to Indonesia. [This speculation is followed by Geertz (1976:231).] Institutions of the kind still exist to date in Hindu India and Buddhist Burma and Thailand (cf. Tebba 1985:269). Since these pesantren-like institutions, if did exist at all, were not Islamic by nature and by function, I do not regard them as part of the pesantren tradition.

[15] In the Middle East, such places are known as *zawiyah* or *khanaqah*. Beginning as "stations" for Sufi followers, these institutions became centres for learning Islam throughout the Middle East.

[16] Tebuireng, a major pesantren studied by Dhofier (1980a), began with a very small *pengajian* group of eight students and Pesantren Ploso, another major pesantren in Kediri, started from a *pengajian* with just five students (Dhofier 1980a:29). Whereas Tebuireng took ten years and Ploso fifty years to become popular as major pesantren (Dhofier, ibid), Daarut Tauhid took only about three years to attract about two thousand followers (*Tempo* 3 April 1993). This might be a reason for the significance of my present study.

[17] This knowledge specialisation of the pesantren tradition has created the *santri* tradition of knowledge-seeking by wandering from one pesantren to another, in order to master to the fullest several branches of Islamic knowledge (Dhofier 1982:24; Bailey 1986:197; Pranowo 1991b:41).

[18] The existence of these two pesantren which concentrate on teaching the Qur'an may revise Dhofier's suggestion that teaching the Qur'an is not the purpose of pesantren system (1980a:59).

[19] Therefore, with the exception of Dhofier's data on *ilmu ladunni* from Garut (1980a:95–96) and on marriage intersections among the *kyai* families that cover Cirebon (1980a:88), Dhofier almost completely neglected West Java. He did not refer to, and thus did not list in his bibliography, Horikoshi's important research on the pesantren tradition in Garut, West Java (1976). This might be due to the unavailability of this work in the library at the time he was writing his thesis.

[20] ITB and Unpad are two of the nine universities of excellence in Indonesia (Raillon 1985:23). This is mainly why Bandung is known as a student city, just like Yogyakarta and Jakarta (Rosyad 1995:2).

[21] This is made possible by the new trend in knowledge transmission practised in Daarut Tauhid, as shall be described later on. This certainly minimises the demand for the provision of *pondok*.

[22] There are interesting features concerning the funding of the construction of the mosque to be discussed later.

[23] *Mazhab* is school of Islamic jurisprudence (*fiqh*). In fact, there were many *mazhab* developed by Muslim *ulama* in accordance with their differing understanding on Qur'an and Hadith. However, to date, only four *mazhab* survive. These are called after their founders: the Hanafi, the Shafi'i, the Maliki, and the Hanbali. They prevail in different parts of Muslim world. The Shafi'i, for example, prevails in Egypt, South Arabia, Syria, East Africa, and Indonesia. Despite this prevailing Shafi'ite school in Indonesia, the modern groups prefer the Hanafi and the Hanbali. This has been the main cause for the modernist-traditionalist dispute in Indonesia.

[24] Detailed discussion of the followers, in terms of their numbers, variety, identity, and reasons for joining, will appear in Chapter Three.

Chapter 2: Initial Stages and Foundation

Officially founded only in 1990, Pesantren Daarut Tauhid was in fact established earlier in 1987 by Abdullah Gymnastiar. This period from 1987 up until 1990 represents the period of the initial stages of the pesantren. There were, during this period, some events which are not merely significant but determinant in the foundation of the pesantren. Echoing Van Gennepian sequences, these events were to a great extent rites de passage, in that they were necessary rites which turned Gymnastiar from an "ordinary persona" into an extraordinary *kyai* (the leader of both the pesantren and many Muslims) and transformed the environment from an ordinary community into a distinguished pesantren milieu.

Furthermore, these events can be seen as a potential foundation and will later explicitly illuminate both the very nature and the primary function of Daarut Tauhid as the *Bengkel Akhlaq* (Workshop for Morality). It will be tangibly apparent in the chapters to follow how these events, with the relative exception of *hajj* and *umrah*, became practised rituals in Daarut Tauhid in fulfilment of its "mission" as the *Bengkel Akhlaq*.

These events were, first, the one-month *i'tikaf* (retreat, stay in a mosque) during Ramadhan and the closely related notion of *lailatul qodar* (the night of power/determinism), secondly the dreams of the Prophet Muhammad, then the *hajj* and *umrah* to Mecca, and finally the *shilaturrahmi* (bonds of friendship). Here I shall respectively describe these events, portraying how they functioned as the preconditions to the foundation of the pesantren and further tracing their significance as rites de passage. But, before doing so, both because K.H. Abdullah Gymnastiar is the key-actor in these events and because he is the key-person as at once the founder and the leader of Daarut Tauhid, I would like first to introduce him.

2.1 The Founder: K. H. Abdullah Gymnastiar

KH. Abdullah Gymnastiar (I shall hereafter name him *Aa Gym* [1] by which he is well-known) is a very young religious leader since he was born in 1962 and only 33 years of age. Being the first-born child of four children, Aa Gym has the characteristic of self-sufficiency and high creativity. Furthermore, early in his childhood, he already showed a talent for leadership. He used to initiate and lead play-groups amongst the children of his own age and even older.

These characteristics of self-sufficiency, creativity, and leadership became more and more apparent throughout his school age growth. Young Aa Gym, and to some extent all his brothers and sister, tend to meet their own needs, both academic and other, without bothering their parents. Aa Gym never asked anything so expensive that his parent could not afford it. If anything, he saved his money and would ask his parent only for the amount he lacked. Concerning this, his mother once imitated for me his words when he wished to buy an expensive pair of shoes: "*Teh*,[2] do you have any spare money?" "What are you after, indeed?" replied his mother. "I wish to buy a pair of shoes but I have only part of money." This begging was however very rarely done by Aa Gym. "Aa Gym never let himself bother me or his father," his mother convinced me. "He and the rest of my children never *merekesel* (force) requested money," she emphasised, "as children commonly do."

This characteristic of self-sufficiency has given rise to another characteristic of Aa Gym, his sense of entrepreneurial business. Early in his primary school period, when he was seven years of age, he had already learned to sell toys such as *kelereng* (marbles), *petasan* (firecracker), and the like. "When attending the first year of primary school," his younger brother once told me, "he used to sell *petasan* to his class- and play-mates." When there was a social event such as a football match, musical show, and the like that attracted a massive crowd of people, he used to sell anything creatively saleable during the occasion.

Aa Gym's parents once in a while attempted to stop this because they worried that it would have a bad impact on his study. Nevertheless, without belittling his parents' concern, he continued his business and succeeded. It is thus evident that the parental apprehension was unnecessary and his parents were eventually proud of Aa Gym's entrepreneurial spirit, which become his inherent characteristic. His parents were particularly proud when these characteristics proved fruitful. By the time Aa Gym graduated from SMP (*Sekolah Menengah Pertama*, Lower Secondary School), he already bought a motorcycle entirely from his own savings. Even more striking was that he could buy a car, again from his own savings, when he graduated from SMA (*Sekolah Menengah Atas*, Upper Secondary School). It is not surprising therefore that he would rely on himself during his tertiary study. He was as capable of meeting his educational fees as other students meet their needs for texts and notebooks. These were all the fruits of his "*bisnis* (business)" activities. "Aa [Gym] *the tiasa milari rizqi sorangan* (Overall, Aa [Gym] has a potent capability to make his own way in life)," concluded his mother. And it was this kind of entrepreneurial talent that brought Aa Gym to his current activities of Islamic entrepreneurship.

Underlying this outstanding characteristic is the fact that Aa Gym was clever as a boy and continues as a brilliant individual. By the time he was three, he could already recite by heart some shortest *surah* (chapters) of the Holy Qur'an. Also by this age he could recite the Latin alphabet from A to Z. It is therefore no surprise that when starting kindergarten he already had the capacity to write and read, commonly only achieved by Sundanese children when they have spent a year or so at primary school.

This intelligence gave Aa Gym special positions throughout his educational career. He was always at the top rank during his school periods at SD (*Sekolah Dasar*, Primary School) and then SMP. "When he graduated from SMP, he was awarded the *juara umum* (best graduate)," his father once told me. Such a distinctive reputation remained unshakeable throughout his SMA-period which qualified him to further his study at the university level.

Aa Gym purportedly used to have a dream to study at ITB (*Institut Teknologi Bandung*, Bandung Institute of Technology). He therefore sat the entry test, which was at that time known as *SIPENMARU* (*Seleksi Penerimaan Mahasiswa Baru*, Entry Selection for New Student), but unfortunately he did not pass and therefore did not gain a place at the institute of his dream.

Interesting to me is the narrative concerning this failure. It is purportedly said that the failure did not at all reflect Aa Gym's incapability for undertaking a study at ITB because he is too clever to fail. Instead, the failure was due to an unfair competition in the process of the test. It was told that when preparing to do the *SIPENMARU*, Aa Gym made an endeavour to do his own preparation.[3] There were some SMA-graduates who joined Aa Gym in this self-study. Lacking academic ability and knowing Aa Gym was a brilliant SMA-student, they asked Aa Gym to guide and teach them.

The results of the *SIPENMARU* were extremely surprising to both Aa Gym and his family. Aa Gym failed while most of his fellows, whose academic ability was "upgraded" by Aa Gym himself, passed. Everyone had the same impression that it was astonishing, suspecting that there was something wrong. There was much speculation as to the reasons for such an unfair decision. One out of Aa Gym's fellows was a son of an influential *pejabat* (governmental authority) in Bandung. The decision might therefore have been "intervened" by a special message from the family of the *pejabat*, as is sometimes the case. Also the test number of this *pejabat*'s son and that of Aa Gym were very close, with only one digit difference. This was believed to make a deliberate exchange not merely possible but also very easy. Based on at least these two reasons, the *SIPENMARU* decision was viewed as unfair and it implied that Aa Gym, as the victim of this unfair competition, was still of high reputation. This narrative plays its own significant contribution in keeping Aa Gym respectable in the eyes of his followers.

Although Aa Gym was unable to attend ITB, he took his place at UNPAD (*Universitas Padjadjaran*, Padjadjaran University) to study accountancy in the Faculty of Economics and Commerce. Accountancy was understandably incompatible with his spirit and thus he resigned from UNPAD after only one year.

Having only spent a year at UNPAD, he transferred to ATA (*Akademi Teknologi Ahmad Yani*, Ahmad Yani Technology Academy) which was renamed UNJANI (*Universitas Jenderal Ahmad Yani*, University of General Ahmad Yani). UNJANI is a private university unlike ITB, which is a public tertiary institute. The common impression is that the former is expensive but not as prestigious as ITB which is nationally prestigious yet inexpensive.

During his time at UNJANI, Aa Gym gained an excellent academic reputation and showed a high level of organisational leadership. He graduated from UNJANI in 1986 with an excellent cum laude record and was chosen as the best graduate of the year. In terms of leadership, he was elected as *ketua senat*, that is, president of the academy-level student association. In fact, Aa Gym had shown this talent for leadership earlier at other schools. He was several times chosen as the KM (*Ketua Murid*, head of students), as he once told me. The students' trust in him to be their leader was a reflection of their admiration of his intelligence and leadership talent. Their trust was based on Aa Gym's intellectual qualities and leadership skill rather than on his physical appearance since he is short and thin. (One metre and fifty-nine in height and about fifty-one kilograms on weight.)

There was a second incident of apparent "bad luck" suffered by Aa Gym besides his failure to attend ITB. His other purported dream was of joining ABRI (*Angkatan Bersenjata Republik Indonesia*, Indonesian Armed Forces). In this case, he wished to follow in his father's footsteps having been heavily influenced by his military environment. His grandfather and father were ABRI officers and Aa Gym grew-up not only in an army family but in the midst of ABRI housing, that is KPAD (*Komplek Perwira Angkatan Darat*, Housing of Army Ground Forces) in Gegerkalong. When at UNPAD, he joined the MENWA (*Resiment Mahasiswa*, Students with Military Training) and he was qualified as a *komandan* (commander), the highest leadership rank in the MENWA.

When taking the entry test for ABRI, he could meet all cognitive requirements to be considered eligible to carry on military training, but, unfortunately, he failed the physical qualification: he lacked a centimetre in height to meet the minimum qualification. As a result, he missed out on his other dream.

These two failures might have left Aa Gym in a state of frustration. His father told me that frustration was seen in Aa Gym's attitude following these failures. His father talked about this when we discussed Aa Gym's motivation in doing *i'tikaf* and in the successive foundation of the pesantren. Such frustration is, I believe, quite understandable if we consider his successful educational career.

Given the two failures with their consequent state of frustration, Aa Gym looked for a place where he could express his feelings and thereby perhaps gain compensation. This place was, to Muslims quite rightly, a neighbouring mosque where he went on retreat observing the so-called *i'tikaf* and hence benefiting from the divine grant of *lailatul qodar*.

2.2 *I'tikaf* and *Lailatul Qodar*

In Islamic *fiqh* (jurisprudence), *i'tikaf* terminologically means to stay in a mosque with a stated *niat* (intention) and in a condition of being *suci* (clean) by the means of doing *wudlu* (ablution) before entering the mosque. *I'tikaf* therefore implies no other rituals than merely staying in the mosque with the condition of being *suci*. Closely related to *i'tikaf, lailatul qadar* etymologically means the night of power or determinism. It is revealed in the Qur'an that there is a single night during the month Ramadhan that is called *lailatul qadar*. On this night, Allah determines the future fate of every human being. This night is therefore so valuable that it is considered by Allah as better than a thousand years (QS. 97:1-5). That a Muslim might be blessed and his fate be a fortunate one he needs to approach Allah. One such way is the *i'tikaf*. To perform *i'tikaf* on the night of power is to be blessed by Allah a thousand fold.

It was in 1987 that Aa Gym stayed in solitude, doing *i'tikaf*, in a neighbouring mosque during Ramadhan 1407 Hijriyya. While Indonesian Muslims usually do *i'tikaf* only during the final ten days of Ramadhan and many of them do it only on the odd days of the ten, Aa Gym did *i'tikaf* during the whole month of Ramadhan. He spent almost the whole day and night in the mosque and "just came home to *buka puasa* (break his fasting) while only rarely coming home to have *sahur* (the dawn meal before fasting)," his parents assured me.

In the mosque Aa Gym did not spend his days complaining to Allah for the failures he was facing, as one might think. Instead, he devoted all the time to performing *shalat*, reciting the holy Qur'an, doing *dzikir* (chanting certain phrases in remembrance or praise of Allah) and *shalawat* (invocation of Allah's mercy for the Prophet Muhammad), and carrying out contemplation in which he did *taubat* (repenting and forswearing). He was making a sincere attempt to know Allah better. All these *i'tikaf* rituals were done to purify himself as part of his effort of *taqorrub ila al-Lah* (approaching Allah).

Performing *shalat* during the *i'tikaf* was to Aa Gym a means by which he could approach the Almighty Allah. He could when performing *shalat* make closer contact with Allah. Indeed, as the very word suggests, *shalat* (prayer!) consists of *do'a* (prayer, invocation)[4] toward the Beneficial Allah. In *shalat*, a Muslim acknowledges the divinity and the might of Allah, to name only some of His honours. Then he asks His forgiveness for all of his sins. Next he begs His blessing and overall guidance for living his worldly life. Such does the "dialogue" between a servant creature and his Absolute Creator continue within the *shalat*. Given such a profound meaning, *shalat* symbolises a high level of piety—regardless of the quality of the *shalat* performed.

Aa Gym therefore performed during his *i'tikaf* more *shalat* than the obligatory ones.[5] He performed many other *shalat sunnat* (optional prayers) that are usually neglected by common Muslims. He diligently performed *shalat lail*, better known as *tahajjud* (optional midnight prayer) when most Muslims are usually sleeping soundly. He also routinely performed *shalat fajar*, an optional prayer preceding *shalat subuh*, *shalat dhuha* (optional prayers performed before noon), *shalat hajat* (prayer service held for the fulfilment of a wish), *shalat taubat* (prayer service held to repent and forswear), and *shalat sunnat qobliyyah* and *ba'diyyah* (overall optional prayers prior to and following the five obligatory payers).

Some of his *i'tikaf* time as well was devoted to reciting the holy Qur'an as a form of sincere dedication to the Merciful Allah. Instead of simply reciting, Aa Gym made an attempt to comprehend the revealed meaning of it. He would therefore recite the holy Qur'an together with its Indonesian translation because he did not at the time fully understand Arabic. However, comprehension itself was not his main goal because in Islam the mere recitation of the Qur'an is a strongly encouraged *ibadah* (act of pure devotion), which brings its own high value of *pahala* (reward, merit) from Allah. As Muslims do, Aa Gym believes that the mere recitation of the Qur'an itself is a valuable *ibadah* while the effort to comprehend it is another form of *ibadah*. At this point, Aa Gym does not follow the reformist's notion that reciting the Qur'an without understanding its meaning is a useless act. During the *i'tikaf*, Aa Gym *khatam* (finished reading) the whole Qur'an several times with the *niat* (intention) of *ibadah*. Besides, he tried grasping the messages of the Qur'an, as another act of *ibadah*, hoping that he could apply its messages to his secular life.

Meditative reflection also assumed a significant part in Aa Gym's *i'tikaf* during the Ramadhan. For this reflection, he had a special room in the mosque. This room was said to be called by his friends as *guha Hiro* (cave Hira). Naming his room such alludes to the prophetic process of the Prophet Muhammad. Cave Hira is the cave near Mecca in which the prophet Muhammad spent much time in spiritual meditation. The prophet is said to have gone on retreat there a month each year meditating on spiritual matters, including conditions in Mecca.

Some parallels can be drawn between these two reflective experiences of Aa Gym and the Prophet Muhammad. This is in no need to raise evidence that Aa Gym is a prophet because, according to Islamic belief, there will be no more prophets sent to earth, the Prophet Muhammad being the last forever. The first parallel is that both the Prophet and Aa Gym went on retreat following the frustration they each faced. The Prophet initially went to the cave when facing the frustration arising from his inability to use his skills and intellectual qualities in trading because of his lack of capital. Aa Gym was driven to reflective *i'tikaf* by the frustration arising from his failure to use his skills and intellectual qualities in realising his dreams. The second parallel is that both were eventually concerned not only with their personal affairs but also with the condition of their communities. The reflection of the Prophet extended from his personal concerns to the malaise in the community of Mecca, especially concerning their polytheistic religious services and intertribal warfare.⁶ Likewise, the personal reflection of Aa Gym extended to the social conditions of the community in Bandung that appeared to him to be deviant from the straight path of Islam. This leads to the third parallel that both are believed to have received a kind of divine message. Both the Prophet and Aa Gym were convinced that their awareness of the social conditions was a message coming from Allah and not the product of their own thinking. This finally resulted in the fourth parallel that both became convinced that they had been called to be the agent of Allah in maintaining religious law and order on the earth. The important point to note here is the predication of the principally distinct agency of these two men; Muhammad is the Prophet, a Messenger of Allah, Aa Gym is a *kyai*, an *ulama* who is the heir of the Prophets.⁷

Returning to the *i'tikaf*, Aa Gym spent a great amount of his *i'tikaf* time, at night in particular, staying in the *guha Hiro* and reflecting upon himself, doing so-called *muhasabah* (introspection) concerning his secular life in this contemporary world. He then came to the belief that whatever failure he was facing was his fault; it originated from his weaknesses. When traced further, he believed, such failure was nothing but the impact of every sin he both intentionally and unintentionally committed. Therefore during the reflection he recalled and acknowledged every sin he might have done and then asked forgiveness from Allah the Forgiver.

This awareness of sin and responsibility for the failure he faced brought Aa Gym to a consciousness of his existence on the earth. The longer his reflection lasted the more conscious he became of his insignificance in the face of the Almighty Allah who created him. He had nothing to be proud of but an abundance of sins engendered by overall negligence of and the subsequent deviance from the *syari'ah* (Islamic path) of Allah. Again, under this acute awareness of his deviance from the straight path, he viewed his failures as a divine "alarm" from none other than Allah.

In the light of this consciousness, he considered that his failures could be conversely viewed as a "success", that would bring him a fortune. Aa Gym came to know that whichever fate Allah determines for him will be for the sake of his *maslahat* (profit, benefit) as he lives in this world. Allah is, Aa Gym believes, Omniscient in such a way that He knows well what is good for him and the reverse. When Allah has predestined that someone "fails" to be an engineer, he exemplified, it is because of Allah's divine knowledge that he is better to "fail"; either because there will be a far better profession than being an engineer, or because it is unbeneficial or even dangerous for him to be an engineer. This conviction of Aa Gym is reflected in this quote:

> Let us learn an example from someone who carried out UMPTN. Say he worked as hard as he could in preparing himself, working together with his classmates by means of forming a study club. As well he said prayers

day and night to Allah. However, Allah's decision was completely out of his expectation. Most of his classmates, whom he helped study, passed the test while he himself, who guided them, failed. Certainly, he could not understand the fact. It is inconceivable that "followers" succeeded whereas their "leader" did not. At the time he could hardly understand the *hikmah* (divine wisdom) behind the scene, he can come to learn it. Praise be to Allah that, while some of his former classmates have become lecturers, he can even deliver *ceramah* (lectures) before lecturers, deans, and counsellors. While some of his former classmates have become soldiers, lieutenant, or captain, he can, by the Will of Allah and wearing "white barret" [Arabic head-cover], even give *pengajian* before majors and generals. So great is the *hikmah* that Allah provided for this person. If we find our face as bitter and a burden, it is simply because either we have not yet recognise a *hikmah* behind it or we tend to claim that our plan is better than Allah's.

This kind of high religious consciousness was achieved by Aa Gym through his reflection during the distinctive occasion of the *i'tikaf*.

Such radical improvement of Aa Gym's religiosity after the *i'tikaf* was said to be the visible evidence of his success in gaining *lailatul qodar*. This was told to me by a religious functionary who said that to gain this means that a Muslim has been granted by Allah a sacred fate for the next year of his life. A Muslim is most likely to gain the *lailatul qodar* if, by the night of power (*lailatul qodar*) he is of the closest relation to Allah, one way of which has been the *i'tikaf*. The concept of obtaining the *lailatul qodar* is in part a matter of coincidence, a Muslim would gain it if the night coincides with his condition of the closest possible relation to Allah. It is believed that, by the night of determination in the year 1407 Hijriyya, Aa Gym's *i'tikaf*, compounded with the various Islamic rituals, gave him a very reasonable chance of gaining the *lailatul qodar*.

In fact, there is no definite "parameter" by which to know whether a Muslim obtains the *lailatul qodar* or not because no one in fact knows the exact night at which the *lailatul qodar* will take place. Muslims only believe that it is but once a year and it is one night out of Ramadhan. Allah does not reveal any exact night in Ramadhan so that it is actually a matter of speculation. Muslim *ulama* estimate that the most likely night must be one of the last ten days of Ramadhan, particularly on the odd dates such as the twenty-first, the twenty-third, and so forth. Given this speculation, it is hard to identify which night coincides with the night of determination.

The only criterion is the post-Ramadhan behavioural performance of any Muslim. If a Muslim acts more pious, showing a higher religious quality, than he had before Ramadhan, it would then most likely be that he gained the *lailatul qodar*. As such, Aa Gym was considered to gain the *lailatul qodar* for he showed a radical change of his religious behaviour, becoming a highly pious Muslim, after passing the month Ramadhan and the *i'tikaf* he exercised therein.[8]

The overall phenomena above provide enough evidence to the view that Aa Gym's *i'tikaf*, with its related *lailatul qodar* is a genuine rite of passage. It radically changed the formerly "ordinary" Aa Gym to an incredibly pious Muslim, who would soon be considered appropriate for the role of a *kyai*.[9] And it was no accident that this presumed *kyai*ship was later legitimised by some dreams involving the prophet Muhammad.

2.3 The Dreams Involving the Prophet Muhammad

Undeniably playing an important part in many cultures, dreams and their interpretation are frequently associated with religious discourses. They are in some cultures believed to be a source of important information regarding the future, the supernatural or spirit world, and religious truth which is not easily provided by ordinary consciousness. This is best exemplified by the shamanistic beliefs in which the dream is perceived as a means of communication with the supernatural world. Likewise, dreams are often believed to reveal aspects of the subjective world and its dynamics in both Western and non-Western cultures, although in the latter they are understandably related to a spiritual world outside the individual (Seymour-Smith 1986:83). In all cases, dreams seem to function as revelatory means.

This function of the dream seems to be apparent in the foundation and later the amazingly rapid growth of Daarut Tauhid. Following the event of *i'tikaf* and the impression of gaining the *lailatul qodar*, there were some dreams believed to reveal to the necessary emergence of Daarut Tauhid and its leader. The dreams were experienced three years before the official foundation of Pesantren Daarut Tauhid. Aa Gym, his relatives, and some of his disciples were said to experience dreams of this kind. These dreams invariably consisted of encounters with the Prophet Muhammad.

> 1. Aa Gym's mother one day experienced a dream in which she came across the Prophet Muhammad who was at the time busy looking for some one. It was unfortunate that she herself did not know whom the Prophet was looking for. She, however, vividly noticed that the Prophet seemed to need someone to whom he wanted to give a sort of instruction.

> 2. A couple of night later Aa Gym's younger brother, Agung, had a dream in which the Prophet Muhammad visited his home. Agung's father asked his elder brother, that is Aa Gym, to welcome the guest, who was none other than the Prophet Muhammad, and have a talk with him. Part of their talk was purportedly the Prophet's deeply-felt concerns over the current situation of Muslims, who seemed to be neglecting some principal pillars of Islamic teachings, such as *shalat*. The Prophet hence

instructed Aa Gym to initiate steps through which he reoriented Muslims by particularly appealing to them to perform *shalat*.

3. Several nights later, it was Aa Gym's turn to experience a dream of this kind. Not only did Aa Gym in his dream see the Prophet Muhammad but he also performed *shalat* together with the Prophet and his immediate companions, namely Abu Bakar, Umar, Utsman, and Ali, who respectively succeeded in the Islamic leadership following the death of the Prophet. Aa Gym said that in the dream, while performing *shalat*, he stood next to Ali while the Prophet himself was the *imam* (head) of the *shalat* performance.

These versions of the dream are cited from *Mangle* (December 1993). There are other dreams with a different story but a slightly similar "message."

4. Agung had a dream that the Prophet Muhammad visited his home. At the time, all members of his family were about to perform *shalat bejamaah* (congregational prayer) at home, as they sometimes do when not going to the mosque. But the Prophet did not join them performing *shalat* on the ground floor. He instead intended to perform *shalat* on the upper level (part of a house that is usually used to dry such things as clothes). Aa Gym's father then asked Aa Gym to see the Prophet saying: "Gym, invite the prophet to perform *shalat* together here and ask his excellency to be the *imam* (head of prayer) for us." Aa Gym then went upstairs. But, instead of coming down with the prophet, Aa Gym strike a *bedug* (large drum usually suspended horizontally at a mosque to summon people to prayer) and made an *Adzan* (call to prayer) upstairs. When coming down, Aa Gym told his father: "The prophet is not pleased to come down. Although it is raining upstairs (the upper level was not roof-covered), the Prophet is rain-proof so that he will not get wet."

5. At another time, Agung had another dream involving Aa Gym. it is said that in the dream Aa Gym was amongst a crowd of people. To Agung's surprise, all the people, except Aa Gym, had monkey-like faces and behaviour. These monkey-like people were one by one lifted-up by Aa Gym, by the means of *dipunggu* (carrying them on his shoulders), to a *menara* (tower of a mosque). From the *menara*, a thundering sound of a massive number of people reciting the Qur'an was heard and a wonderfully bright light was seen illuminating the surroundings.

6. Aa Gym had a dream in which he was visited by an old man in a clean, white Arabic-styled garment. The old man daubed a kind of honey, using a chicken feather, over Aa Gym's face, telling him that Aa Gym would be a noble person in the future.

7. Abdurrahman Yuri, the second-born in the family, had another dream again involving the Prophet Muhammad. Yuri told me in an interview that he can always vividly remember the dream and wishes to experience again a dream of that kind. In the dream, he was engaged in a war in a valley together with the Prophet and his companions. He was safeguarding the Prophet Muhammad against any attack from the enemy.

Before further analysing these dreams, I would like to introduce the key-person who experienced the seminal dream. The story of the dream, relating to the foundation of Daarut Tauhid, centres on Agung, Aa Gym's younger brother, both because he was the most frequent individual who dreamt and because of the fact that almost all the dreams, experienced by others, were in some ways related to him.

Agung, the third born son, had suffered from paralysis years before he passed away at age 25 in 1991. During those years, many uninvited volunteers took care of him. According to Agung's brother Yuri nearly everyone of the volunteers miraculously experienced a dream, or dreams, in which they encountered the Prophet Muhammad. Hakim, a volunteer, was one day found by Aa Gym's mother crying beside Agung. Aa Gym's mother surprisedly asked Hakim what happened to him. Hakim, with teardrops trickling down his cheeks, answered: "Mother, I am happy. I just encountered the Prophet Muhammad in my dream." "But I did not see you sleeping?" wondered the mother. "Well, I fell asleep on the feet of Aa Agung while I was looking after him," explained Hakim. This is just an example of how someone related to Agung could have a dream involving the Prophet. It was then believed that, when Agung's mother, Aa Gym, and Yuri saw the Prophet in their dreams, it was to a great extent a *hikmah* (divine wisdom) from having a very close relation with and taking care of Agung.

By no means had Agung become Allah's agent in helping others see the Prophet in a dream. It is believed that it is not Agung himself who "generated" that kind of the dream but it was the others' kindness in helping Agung survive which brought forth these dreams. In light of the notion of *hikmah* and *amal shaleh* (pious deed), it is believed that one will always benefit somehow from whatever kindness one does. Taking care of Agung was so valuable an *amal shaleh* that one would be surely worthy of gaining a subsequent reward. Since Agung missing out on physical enjoyment due to his paralysis enjoyed several dreams with the Prophet, the reciprocal was that these others could share the enjoyment of having a dream of the Prophet. Put another way, Agung was a passive medium through which one, providing he was kind enough toward Agung, might be able to see the Prophet in a dream.

Agung was also viewed as a passive channel for the transmission of *baraka* (divine blessing). Hakim is believed to be one of those who enjoyed the *baraka* transmitted through Agung when he achieved great success in school. This success was, it is believed, a manifestation of *baraka* for his kindness in offering himself to tend Agung, bathing him and even helping him to defecate and urinate.[10]

Furthermore, it was believed that Agung's physical paralysis had no any impact on his human feeling and thinking. His mother even suspected whether what Agung suffered was a paralysis at all because she believes that, up until the last day, Agung's feelings remained active, even better than others'. According to Yuri, the paralysis made no impact on Agung's heart and mind, indicating no memory loss. "He was visited by many people coming to ask him for *do'a* or mere wisdom." Yuri said. Hence it is clear that Agung was thought of by many as deserving the authority of being a passive medium via which the *hikmah* and *baraka* might be gained.

This conviction contributed a considerable significance to the way people viewed the dreams Agung told. The dreams were viewed as *ru'ya shadiqah* (true dreams) which can be experienced only by such sinless and pious Muslims as Agung. In relation to this, an informant quotes two Hadith:

> "The believers' vision is a forty-sixth part of prophecy."

> "Naught is now left of prophecy but the bearers of good tidings." The companions asked: "What are the bearer of good tidings?" The Prophet said: "They are the visions of the pious."

All dreams experienced by the Prophet Muhammad were *ru'ya shadiqah* and the Prophet would only come in *ru'ya shodiqoh* that are experienced by Muslims. The presence of the Prophet in a dream itself is believed to be the sign of a revelatory dream as hinted in the Hadith. So, those dreams related to Daarut Tauhid appear to be profoundly revelatory.

The second dream, for instance, reveals that the Prophet Muhammad, in his visit to Aa Gym's family, directly gave instruction to Aa Gym to do a sort of prophetic job. The Prophet, being deeply concerned about the current condition of Muslims who tended in the eyes of the Prophet to be deviating from an Islamic course, asked Aa Gym to turn Muslims back to the path of Islam. Since *shalat* is the pillar of Islam, this instruction was symbolised by appealing to Muslims to perform at least the five obligatory *shalat*. Worth noting here is that the Prophet's direct command was to Aa Gym, neither to any of his brothers or sister nor to his parents. This served as an explicit legitimation for Aa Gym. It was tangibly Aa Gym who was to be the heir of the Prophet, not anyone else.

The fourth dream revealed similar messages with a slightly different story. Again, *shalat* appears to be the main issue here; Aa Gym's family were about to perform *shalat* when the Prophet came intending to perform *shalat* in Aa Gym's family's house. *Shalat* seems even more crucial when the sound of *bedug* and *adzan*, features inherently related to *shalat*, occurred in the story. Furthermore, the symbolic function of *shalat* is stronger here since there were no verbal instruction made by the Prophet, unlike that in the first dream. And again, Aa Gym was the key-actor being the only person who saw the Prophet, sounded the *bedug*, and announced the *adzan*. That the Prophet refused to go downstairs is not to prove that he is water-proof but to have a chance to talk privately to Aa Gym as they did in the first dream. This is another explicit statement of legitimacy for Aa Gym.

The symbolic function of *shalat* and the legitimacy for Aa Gym were reinforced further through the third dream. In this dream, the Prophet Muhammad practically symbolised the way of correcting Muslims by performing *shalat* together with his main four companions and Aa Gym himself. The involvement of Aa Gym in the *shalat* performance is an absolute statement of legitimacy for him to be considered one of the heirs of the Prophet, inheriting the prophet's job on earth, but not the prophethood. This is strengthened by another feature that Aa Gym was next to Ali in the *shalat* performance. Ali was the youngest of the earliest converts to Islam by the Prophet. Ali is therefore a symbol of the young devout Muslim. So when it is portrayed that Aa Gym and Ali stood side by side in the *shalat*, Aa Gym is associated with Ali, in that he should be, as Ali was, a young devout Muslim sacrificing his life for the spread and the maintenance of Islam as a world religion. Moreover the presence of the four *khulafa al-rasyidin* (the guiding Vice Regents) symbolises the continuity of post-Muhammad leadership. These four Vice Regents were considered the legitimate post-Muhammad leaders. Being together with them, Aa Gym might thus be considered to inherit directly their authority of leadership.

The religious role of Aa Gym is further depicted in the fifth dream. The crowd of monkey faced people is thought of as an image of the great majority of contemporary Muslims who tend to deviate from the Islamic path. As in the Qur'an or Hadith, the animal-like performance is often used as a symbol of deviation and sinfulness. That crowd is thus a crowd of sinful Muslims. Aa Gym came there to reorient them. This reorientation is symbolised by transporting the people one by one to the *menara* of the mosque where devout Muslim were reciting the Qur'an. The mosque, the thunderous recitation of the Qur'an and the very bright light all symbolise the straight path and the *nur* (divine light) of Islam. Conspicuous here is the certain impression of the religious authority and competence of Aa Gym. And this is of course another potential source of legitimacy.

Those dreams demonstrate twin functions; legitimative and instructive. The dreams are legitimative in the sense that they, with great efficacy, convinced Muslims that they would have a *kyai*. Those dream are instructive as well in the sense that they convinced Aa Gym, personally, and his family that he had been chosen by Allah to be His agent in reorienting Muslims to the straight path of Islam.

Why were those Muslims convinced by the dreams since we know not all dreams are legitimative? Mainly because these dreams involved the Prophet and were followed by the fact that Aa Gym experienced a fundamental transformation of religiosity and that he was suddenly driven by Allah to perform *hajj* and *umrah*. Furthermore, the dreams were made public first by Agung, Agung's volunteer tenders, the visitors to Agung, his family, and later by the mass media and Aa Gym's public talks. Thus, the significance of those dreams was judged by what followed immediately, just like we can see from many cases in the history of Java (Fox 1991:29). People at Daarut Tauhid believe that the meaning of the dreams is what they are witnessing: the extraordinary leadership of Aa Gym and the establishment of the pesantren.

Photograph 2 Aa Gym, the dreams, and the foundation of the pesantren as published by *Mangle*, a local magazine[11]

2.4 The *Hajj* and The *Umrah*

The *hajj* is the Muslims' greater pilgrimage to the holy places of Mecca and Madina. It is performed annually between the eighth and thirteenth days of Dzul Hijja, the twelfth month of Hijriyya. Being the fifth of the five pillars of Islam, the *hajj* is conceived of as the final religious duty that every well-to-do

Muslim is required to perform at least once in a lifetime. It is not, however, an obligation for those Muslims who do not have the capacity, economical or physical, to do so.

Meanwhile, the *umrah* is the Muslims' lesser pilgrimage to those places. It is lesser in value because, while the *hajj*, being the fifth pillar of Islam, is *wajib* (obligatory), the *umrah* is only *sunnah* (optional, but meritorious if performed). It is also lesser because, while the *hajj* is an event of millions of attendant Muslims in Mecca at a certain time, the *umrah* is prescribed for Muslims at any time of the year, so that it is not a massive occasion. Notwithstanding its importance, the *umrah* shares many features of the *hajj*.

Aa Gym performed his first *hajj* in 1407 Hijriyya, or 1987 A.D., not long after the *i'tikaf* in the preceding Ramadhan and after the revealing and guiding dreams. He did the pilgrimage to Mecca together with his beloved mother. Unlike other Muslims who usually plan the *hajj* long before departure, it is said that Aa Gym did not plan the *hajj* except briefly a few days before departure. It occurred suddenly and unpredictably and required immediate attention without a long planned itinerary. If anything, this instant itinerary is seen as divine not human as is clear from the following belief. According to his mother, this suddenness was a sign of the will of Allah in driving them to Mecca. She said: "I was purely granted by the Almighty Allah to undertake the *hajj*. We had a dream in which we encountered the Prophet and we were driven to Mecca by the divine plan of Allah."

Indeed, it was this nuance of suddenness which made this experience of *hajj* extraordinarily valuable to Aa Gym himself, his mother, the rest of his family, and his future followers. This idea of a sudden occurrence gave rise to an impression fundamental to the emergence of Daarut Tauhid and its initiator. As were the dreams of the Prophet, this sort of impression facilitated in Aa Gym a fundamental confidence that he would become an agent of Allah in the mission of *i'lai kalimatillah* (upholding the law of Allah) amongst the recent generation of Muslims. This was why, it is believed, Allah granted him an unexpected opportunity to do the pilgrimage to Mecca, an expensive chance that costs so much.[12] Thus, Aa Gym saw a divine message from the sudden *hajj*. This sudden occurrence of Aa Gym's *hajj* also inculcated a significant trust in his family and the followers of the divine agency personally entrusted to Aa Gym. He is, to them, the 'delegate'—not to say the 'messenger' which might be misconceived of as the prophet—of Allah to bring them back from any deviance to the *shirat mustaqiem* (straight path) of Islam. Thus this suddenness in conducting the *hajj* made its own considerable contribution to building the image of the *kyai*ship of Aa Gym and, it follows, of his competency to found a kind of pesantren. This is because, unlike in the past, simply being a *haji* (pilgrim)[13] no longer means being a *kyai* or religious leader. In the past, the early generation of Indonesian *haji* used to be, as soon as they returned from the *hajj*, a leading Muslim or a *kyai* (Geertz 1969:205, 1995:81). Now, this is no longer the case with Indonesian *haji*. The returning *haji* tend to remain ordinary in that they become neither a *kyai* nor in any sense a religious leader. So, what facilitated Aa Gym's position of *kyai*ship was not merely his being a *haji* but also the inherent notion of divine instruction to fulfil it, evident through its sudden occurrence without Aa Gym's initiative.

Such an impression of divine "intervention" always accompanied the occasion of Aa Gym's performance of either the *hajj* and *umrah*. At the time I was doing fieldwork, he had already undergone the *hajj* five times and the *umrah* three times, the most recent was at the time I was there. This high frequency was striking to everyone, including myself because he and his parents do not seem rich enough to afford such a frequency. This of course gives rise to the "suspicion" of some sort of "outside" intervention. Inevitably, such an "outside" intervention has been reckoned to be a divine one, partly due to divine instruction, partly because Aa Gym is valued as an extraordinarily pious Muslim, even a *kyai*, and partly based on the guiding dreams.

This belief is justified by the narrative concerning the cost of the *hajj*. I was told by Aa Gym himself and his mother that for some the divine plan is tangible in terms of the cost of doing the *hajj*. "The money to pay ONH always comes so smoothly without any trouble as though it comes from nowhere," said his mother. It happened that an anonymous person paid the ONH as soon as Aa Gym had booked. His mother said: "We did not have any idea at all who he was but he rang us to say that the ONH was paid. And not long afterwards we were delivered, again from the anonymous sender, all the equipment necessary to undergo the *hajj*, such as bags and *pakaian ihram* (special clothing worn during the *hajj* to Mecca)." Although this phenomenon can be understood as a matter of a social gift, presuming that such an anonymous "kind" person might be either Aa Gym's closest friend or a member of his adherent *jamaah*, the overwhelming notion here remains of divine intervention. That is due to the belief that, even if the case is one of a gift, it is no more than Allah's way of applying His absolute will. If Allah wished, Aa Gym believes, He can absolutely prompt the anonymous person to pay the costs of the *hajj*.

While on his first *hajj*, Aa Gym with his mother stayed in Mecca and Madina for forty days. Despite the particular *hajj* rituals, what Aa Gym did during his stay in those holy places more or less resembled what he did during his one-month of *i'tikaf* time in Bandung. Indeed, doing *i'tikaf* at *Masjid al-Haram* (the Great Mosque) in Mecca is, as one might certainly imagine, remarkably more advantageous than at any other mosque in the world.

Aa Gym therefore spent most of his days in Mecca at *Masjid al-Haram* in *i'tikaf*. He spent only a few moments at his home-stay. In the Great Mosque, he observed such rituals as *shalat*, both the obligatory five and, even more excessively, the optional ones. He did a lot of *dzikir* and *shalawat* as well as the recitation of the holy Qur'an. He also made a considerable attempt to do *istigfar* (ask for Allah's forgiveness) and *taubat*, under the belief that *istigfar* and *taubat* are most acceptable if done in the holy place of Mecca, more particularly next to the *ka 'bah* (cubicle shrine in the centre of the Great Mosque). Reflection was also an immensely important part of his businesses during the *i'tikaf* in *Masjid al-Haram*. In short, Aa Gym's activities in Mecca, besides the specific rituals of *hajj*, were a further intensification of what was done during the *i'tikaf* in Indonesia.

There are of course some distinguishing features between performing similar rituals in Mecca and that in one's own home-country. Mecca itself is held to be the holy place where the divine rewards for any performance of *ibadah* is not only doubled or tripled but increased thousands and thousands of times. The *Masjid al-Haram*, the *ka 'bah* at the centre of it, the *multajam* (a certain part of the Great Mosque) next to it, and the *maqam Ibrahim* (Abraham shrine) beside it, to name some features, are firmly believed to make any *ibadah* performed there profoundly valuable, one's *istigfar* and *taubat* most likely accepted, and one's *do'a* most possibly heard. The *multajam* is, most particularly, held to be the most sacred place where nearly all Muslims' *do'a* is fulfilled by Allah. These features brought about the principal transformation of Aa Gym's personality and religiosity.

The particular *hajj* rituals had immense importance in such a transformation. Performing *hajj* is, to Aa Gym, *perjalanan ma'rifatullah* (a voyage of gnosis), meaning that all *hajj* rituals comprise certain symbols for purifying one's self, as a way of approaching Allah in order to know Him well and thus at once love and obey Him. When stoping at *Miqat*,[14] for example, pilgrims replace their daily clothes with *pakaian ihram*. Here the pilgrims, according to Aa Gym, intend the replacement of any *pakaian maksiat* (irreligious behaviour) by *pakaian taat* (religious conduct); such bad characteristics as *riya* (showing off), *nifaq* (hypocrisy) are to be replaced by such good ones such as *ikhlas* (sincerity), *jujur* (honesty) and so forth. Taking the bath at the Miqat means freeing oneself from any previous sins. Declaring *niat* in performing the *hajj* at Miqat extends to the pilgrims' intention in their lifetime to stop doing any *haram* (forbidden) acts, in accordance with Islamic teachings.[15] The pilgrims' performance of two-*raka'at* (cycles of prayer)[16] in *shalat* symbolises their intention of *taqorrub* (approaching) Allah because, to Him, *shalat* is the most favoured *ibadah* (dedication) a Muslim does. After the Miqat, a pilgrim's concentration on *hajj* rituals symbolises his sincere dependence and reliance on none other than Almighty Allah. Saying *talbiyah*[17] symbolises not merely a pilgrim's fulfilment of Allah's call in performing *hajj* but the fulfilment of the totality of Islamic teachings. The ultimate goal is not merely the fulfilment of an obligation but the achievement of Allah's *keridoan* (favour). Likewise, performing *thawaf* (the ritual of circumambulation of the Ka'bah seven times) and reenacting *sa'i* (slow and desperate running back and forth between Shofa and Marwah) symbolise a pilgrim's effort to run closer to Allah to achieve His *keridoan*.

For Aa Gym, to touch the *Hajar Aswad* symbolises hand shaking with Allah, by which Allah does the pilgrim honour and blesses him with mercy. In consequence, he/she has to keep himself pure from any sin and disobedience against Allah's law, otherwise Allah will withdraw the divine honour and blessing gained through the "hand shaking". *Wukuf* (the ritual of gathering on the desert of Arafah during the *hajj*) is a field where the pilgrim can intensively improve his/her *ma'rifat* by means of reflection focusing on the almighty power of Allah symbolised by the large area of Arafah and the large number of pilgrims gathering there. At the same time the pilgrim reflects on the omniscience of Allah that He knows perfectly all that one does, all that one feels, and whatever one has in mind.[18]

Aa Gym did his best in performing all these *hajj* rituals and they deeply affected his personal behaviour. The transformation of his personal religiosity after the *hajj* was much greater than after the *i'tikaf*. He became more intense in performing Islamic rituals and more strict in reinforcing Islamic law in his day-to-day life. Here it is evident the degree to which the *hajj* is a rite de passage as suggested, for one, by Michael Wolfe who writes: "The Hadj [*hajj*] is a shared rite of passage. I saw it through the eyes of others as much as through my own…" (qtd. in Eaton 1995:291). This is most tangibly shown in the case of Aa Gym. After fulfilling the *hajj*, Aa Gym who had no background of Islamic education, such as one would receive in a pesantren, later became worthy of being a *kyai* and capable of founding a pesantren.

To mark this immensely significant change, Aa Gym renamed himself by adding a more "Islamic" name to his former one.[19] Before performing his first *hajj*, his name was just Gymnastiar.[20] Now, his full name became Abdullah Gymnastiar, the Abdullah being added in Mecca when performing his first *hajj*. The first name was proudly given to him by the *imam besar* (great leader) of the Great Mosque in Mecca. There is an interesting story concerning the process by which the name was given.

> It was on a Friday that Aa Gym asked an *asykar* (security guard) to help him obtain a name from the *imam*. As there is a hierarchical procedure, made up of several *asykar*, to reach the *imam*, the *asykar* then asked another *asykar* to tell the next *asykar* and so forth till the request reached the *imam*. In portraying this hierarchical procedure, his mother told me: "There are layers of safeguarding *asykar* around the *imam* as though the *imam* is more difficult to reach than a president would be." Surprisingly, while he usually simply gives a name for a pilgrim through his *asykar*,

> the *imam* called Aa Gym personally. Then he whispered to Aa Gym giving the name; Abdullah. More startlingly, the *imam* publicly announced Aa Gym's new name so that all the pilgrims who were present, including the *asykar*, repeatedly echoed the name. At the same time, the *asykar* rushed up congratulating and kissing Aa Gym. While coming home, Aa Gym cried in front of his mother when he told her the story.

This story epitomises the honours Aa Gym was beginning to receive. Abdullah was the name of the father of the Prophet Muhammad. The name Abdullah, etymologically meaning the *'abd* (servant) of Allah, indicates Aa Gym to be a fully pious *'abd* of Allah, a high honour that every Muslim would wish to obtain. Next, the personal encounter with the Great *Imam* of *Masjid al-Haram* was another honour, legitimising Aa Gym as a future leader of Muslims. This was further demonstrated by the salute and congratulations from the pilgrims and *asykar*.

Aa Gym came home to Indonesia with a remarkable transformation of his personality and religiosity even more than what he had obtained from the *i'tikaf* in Ramadhan. The *i'tikaf* and its outcome, the dreams involving the Prophet and their interpretation, and the *hajj* with its transformative results altogether convinced Aa Gym of his representation of divine agency—particularly his *kyai*ship. This was a culmination of an awareness he had felt earlier during Ramadhan. One day in Ramadhan, he surprised his father, who was fixing a car in front of the house, by saying: "*Pa* (Dad), I wish to be an *ulama*."[21] Given goal, compounded with awareness of his lack of the Islamic knowledge necessary to be a *kyai*, Aa Gym began doing the so-called *Shilaturrahmi*.

2.5 The *Shilaturrahmi*

Aa Gym knew he ought to seek deeper Islamic knowledge through such competent sources as the *ulama*. He therefore started visiting Islam's leading *kyai*, those whom he considered representative of.

Aa Gym began his visits with some of *ulama sepuh* (elderly *ulama*). The first was a *kyai* of advanced age in Garut, a town to the east of Bandung. After introducing himself and explaining his lack of Islamic knowledge and his recent strange experiences, Aa Gym asked the *kyai*'s assistance to instruct him in Islamic matters. The *kyai* transmitted his knowledge to Aa Gym in a brief encounter only, further guiding him to see K. H. Khoer Affandi, the leader of the pesantren Miftahul Huda at Manonjaya, Tasikmalaya, a neighbouring town to Garut. This latter *kyai* then became Aa Gym's primary instructor until he passed away in November 1994. His influence on Aa Gym is evident, marked by the major orientation of Aa Gym's Islam with the emphasis on *tauhid* (oneness of Allah) and *akhlaq* (morality) and the choice of the very name of the pesantren; *Daarut Tauhid* (the hamlet of *tauhid*). Pesantren throughout Indonesia, while trying to cover all aspects of Islamic teaching, still have their own specialisation, each focusing on certain branches of Islamic studies such as *Nahwu and Shorof* (Arabic linguistics), *Tafsir* (Commentary on Qur'an), *Hadith* (Recorded traditions of the Prophet), *Tauhid, Akhlaq, Mantiq* (Logics) and so forth. *Tauhid* and *Akhlaq* are the "trademark" of K. H. Khoer Affandi's pesantren, Miftahul Huda, as are they of Aa Gym's pesantren, Daarut Tauhid.[22]

Aa Gym was in a sense the *santri* (student) of K. H. Khoer Affandi. However, he was an extraordinary santri in that instead of *masantren* (staying at pesantren) at Miftahul Huda for years as santri usually do he simply visited K. H. Khoer Affandi for some hours at a time during which he acquired his knowledge. These visits were irregular and simply followed the "mood" of Aa Gym; he visited the *kyai* whenever he felt the need to, although he most frequently did it on Wednesday nights.

What is the nature of the knowledge transmission involved, for it is inconceivable that during such brief encounters the knowledge transmission would be as conventional in nature as the ordinary educational systems? Private instruction might well go on at those times during which Aa Gym had a private meeting with K. H. Khoer Affandi, but no source has so far suggested such an occasion. What usually went on, so far as I was informed, were ordinary conversations between K. H. Khoer Affandi, often accompanied by his family, and Aa Gym, usually accompanied by his family, disciples, or *ajudan* (guardian).[23] The conversations were therefore both ordinary and open in nature, without any sense of privacy. K. H. Khoer Affandi convinced Aa Gym and companions, during their visits, that he did not need to teach Aa Gym anything because "the knowledge you [Aa Gym] are seeking is available in your self, granted by Allah. Or, otherwise, it will sooner or later come to you." Then, is it the case that this strange transmission of knowledge was related to the personal quality of Aa Gym?

Indeed, Aa Gym believed that these visits were naturally rich sources of knowledge. What he saw, heard, or felt during such visits were an immensely valuable training providing he was capable enough of apprehending the lessons. *How* a *kyai* acts, speaks, and generally behaves is, to Aa Gym, a most valuable lesson applicable to any Muslim's daily life. This does not yet take into account *what* a *kyai* says, which is another part of such a lesson. Aa Gym even extended the possibilities of such lessons by suggesting that they could quite possibly be taken from other ordinary people, not just *kyai*. He exemplified this, in a public sermon I attended, as follows.

> I [Aa Gym], on a way to visit a friend, saw two people talking to each other. I heard that one of them was expressing his feeling of regret following his loss of a certain amount of money, stolen by a pick-pocket. He moaned and told the other what happened, crying for help or any

suggestion on how to get the money back. The other's response was more advanced than my thinking at that time. He readily said: "Money is rubbish. Nothing to regret." The man who lost the money was dramatically calmed down by this "advice." I took an unexpected lesson from this phenomenon. The point I noted was the phrase "money is rubbish." Maintaining this attitude towards money and all other kinds of wealth is important in keeping ourselves calm especially during those times of financial troubles. This is an important lesson in self-control that is frequently needed in many tense situations. Furthermore, while we consider that money is important to our lives, this "money is rubbish" attitude must be incorporated into our character so we do not fall to serving money and thereby forgetting Allah who provides us with any wealth.

The above example demonstrates how Aa Gym seeks knowledge. And so his knowledge acquisition during his visits to the *ulama* occurred in a similar fashion.

Benefiting from this manner of knowledge acquisition, Aa Gym continues to visit as many *ulama* as possible. He calls such visits part of the *shilaturrahmi*.[24] He visits both those who lead pesantren, mostly well known as *kyai*, and those who lead Islamic activities at universities. He also visits both modernist and traditionalist *ulama*. This is in accordance with his inclination to "reconcile" various groups of Muslims, which are often trapped in religious disputes. For this, his orientation of Islam is known as *mazhab shilaturrahmi* (*Tempo* April 3, 1993).

This tradition of *shilaturrahmi* visits to leading *kyai* is critical to Aa Gym being credited as a *kyai*, particularly because of his lack of Islamic training. Further, this *shilaturrahmi* tradition can be seen as an elaboration of the concept of *wasilah* (chain of knowledge transmission), a common feature in the *ziarah* visit) tradition among Muslims (Jamhari 1995:2). To visit a *kyai* or a *wali* (saint), either alive or dead, is a means by which to link the visitor to the visited and ultimately to the Prophet who is regarded as the closest one to Allah (van Bruinessen 1992:75). Using different terminology, Zamakhsyari Dhofier, labelling such visits as *rihla ilmiya* (study tour) and *wasilah* as *isnad* (intellectual chain), found such visits as a prominent practice among *kyai* and *santri* in Java. They thus acquired *isnad* to legitimate the authenticity of their knowledge (1982:79). Although Aa Gym did not intend his *shilaturrahmi* tradition to gain such formal *isnad*, his visits to leading Muslim leaders provided a profound contribution to his *kyai*ship. That Aa Gym visits many *kyai* has become, among his followers, a public discourse that strengthens Aa Gym's status of *kyai*ship. Some followers told me, for example, that Aa Gym also has a "guide" in Demak, a *ziarah* centre of *wali* tombs (see Fox 1991).

Left: Photograph 3 Aa Gym after the performance of the *hajj*: devoutly pious. Right: Photograph 4 Aa Gym is known for promoting the *shilaturrahmi* orientation (taken from *Tempo* April 3, 1993).

Another aspect of this *shilaturrahmi* tradition at Daarut Tauhid is to visit non-religious institutions, where people can learn such useful knowledge as the activities and overall management system needed in organising the pesantren, in particular its economic activities. Therefore, Aa Gym's *shilaturrahmi* covers both religious and "secular" figures, so that it contributes both religious and "secular" knowledge. At this point, the *shilaturrahmi* becomes a sort of comparative study, useful both to the improvement of Aa Gym's knowledge personally and to the overall development of Daarut Tauhid.

In conclusion, the *shilaturrahmi* has become a means by which Aa Gym improves his knowledge both religious (Islamic) and non-religious. With his mental capability he finds the *shilaturrahmi* fruitful as a means of knowledge acquisition so that he does not feel it necessary to *masantren*. These visits contribute so much to the improvement of Aa Gym's knowledge, particularly Islamic knowledge, that he felt himself qualified to found an Islamic centre such as a pesantren.

2.6 The Foundation of Daarut Tauhid

The embryo of Pesantren Daarut Tauhid began when a couple of teenagers, who were high school students, asked Aa Gym to deliver a *ceramah keagamaan* (religious speech) at their school, SMA-3 of Bandung. These teenagers would never have asked Aa Gym to do something like that before Aa Gym had done *i'tikaf* and undertaken the *hajj*. They recognised the authority of Aa Gym to give them religious advice since they witnessed the radical changes in Aa Gym's personality and religiosity. They also heard of the revealing dreams of the Prophet Muhammad, experienced by Aa Gym himself and his family, which contributed to their confidence in Aa Gym.

Aa Gym's speech was so successful in impressing his audience, who were all SMA-3 students, that they asked him to come there on a monthly basis. Yet this frequency was not satisfactory to some of the audience. They then set up a weekly *pengajian* at Aa Gym's home, during which they listened to Aa Gym's advice concerning religious matters. Those attending steadily grew week by week, occupying only a small room in Aa Gym's house, then its main room, next its garage, and later its front yard and even the street. From no more than ten attendants at the beginning, in late 1987, it drew a following of about 400 people by 1989.

Initially the *pengajian* was informally organised by those pioneering SMA-students. Then, as the number of *jemaah* grew, it was formally organised by the so-called KMIW (*Kelompok Mahasiswa Islam Wiraswasta*, Islamic Student Group for Entrepreneurship). This group, as the name suggests, was in fact set up by Aa Gym and some of his friends to develop economic activities, under the banner of Islam and thus implementing an Islamic system of economy. The group was active in silk-screening and printing services. It consisted of Aa Gym, his brother and sister, and a few friends. The group then found the weekly *pengajian* to play an important part in their activities, which were viewed to serve the spiritual and ethical needs of their businesses ventures.

Aa Gym began to find the space for the weekly *pengajian* at his parent's home in Gegerkalong Hilir limited. They then took the initiative to look for a larger and more strategic place. These were some rooms in Gegerkalong Girang whose surrounding yards were wide enough for a huge gathering. They rented the rooms to live in as well as a centre for their activities.

As time went, the *pengajian* became more popular and about eight hundred Muslims attending. The *pengajian* itself was by then popularly known as the *Pengajian Tauhid*; a religious sermon that focused on intensive comprehension and application of *tauhid* as the basis for the enhancement of Islamic morality.

Photograph 5 Tents were built to accommodate the massive number of followers.

Given the massive following, Aa Gym felt it necessary to set up a formal institution and organise the *pengajian*. On September the fourth 1990, Aa Gym and the KMIW therefore founded a *yayasan* (foundation) called *Yayasan Daarut Tauhid*, with Aa Gym as its chairman. The foundation of the *yayasan* was accordingly the official foundation of Pesantren Daarut Tauhid, formalising the *pengajian* activities that had been ongoing since late 1987. The *yayasan* form was chosen because it encompasses both religious and economic activities and provides the legal and formal requirements for those activities.[25]

The foundation of Pesantren Daarut Tauhid was viewed by Aa Gym and his companions as the Will of Allah. Asked about the emergence of the pesantren, he replied:

> There is great curiosity about Daarut Tauhid, and many people have asked me how we have accomplished so much. They said that they find Daarut Tauhid very amazing in its rapid development. According to them, not all pesantren grew as rapidly as Daarut Tauhid. Others were also amazed by the fact that Daarut Tauhid achieved this success of rapid growth but never begged for donations or any other forms of funding from others. My answer to these kinds of question is always, and will always be, one: all these things happen by the Will of Allah. I and my friends here are merely His Creatures which He sets in His motion to operate these things.

People at Daarut Tauhid point to many occurrences that prove this is the Will of Allah. Aa Gym's spiritual progress since 1987, involving *i'tikaf*, true visions, and pilgrimage to Mecca, is an often mentioned proof. Another proof is the emergence of KMIW. The establishment of this group implies that, in the first place, Aa Gym did not think in terms of a pesantren. At the time he just thought to form a group that puts together Muslims with similar interests, that is entrepreneurial activities, under the spirit of Islam. Therefore, that Aa Gym and his fellows came to the decision to found a pesantren institution in 1990 was perceived as their being led by the Will of Allah. The final proof is the bizarre funds Daarut Tauhid enjoys in funding its development. Donations came anonymously. They came either in the form of money or building materials. It is believed that these bizarre funds were sent over by pious Muslims, who donated in the name of Allah. This truly demonstrates the Will of Allah in developing Daarut Tauhid.

In deciding its direction, Daarut Tauhid has formulated the philosophical principles that have become the bases for its activities and have served as its main objective. Daarut Tauhid is set up to produce a Muslim community with three main characteristics:

1) *Ahli Dzikir*. A Muslim who always strives to do *dzikir* (remember Allah) in the ways taught by Islam. By doing so, the Muslim will certainly have the closest relationship with Allah, a stand that makes him strong, stable, and calm in facing any situation in life because of his confidence in Allah's promises of supporting and helping His beloved people. The Muslim will always be enthusiastic and never give up because of his belief that doing his best is part of the *ibadah* that Allah likes so much.

2) *Ahli Pikir*. A Muslim who pursues the custom of reflection and contemplation of every phenomenon he faces. By this, the secrets of life will be unveiled, hidden potential unleashed, and *hikmah* (lesson, wisdom) of problems and happenings revealed. Given these advantages, the Muslim will always be in the best position to face any challenge and solve any problem, either personally with himself or communally with the wider Muslim *ummat*.

3) *Ahli Ikhtiar*. A Muslim who follows the custom of hard work while living in this world, as a result of *dzikir* and *pikir*, through the actions allowed by Allah the Almighty. In this way, the Muslim will be a productive and creative person with credible achievements.

The foundation of Daarut Tauhid drew both positive and negative responses although the former was immensely stronger. The positive response was clearly demonstrated by the *pengajian* attendants. The massive number of *pengajian* attendants made large donations to support the financial necessities of building the pesantren. No less than four hundred thousand rupiahs would be collected at each single *pengajian*. Besides, many individuals made their own separate donations in the form of either money or materials. These certainly accelerated the development of Pesantren Daarut Tauhid.

Negative response came mainly from neighbouring religious specialists, particularly because they doubted the piety of Aa Gym and his capacity and competence to be a *kyai*. Such doubt was prompted by their claim that Aa Gym once belonged to an *anak kolong* gang, a group of ABRI-children who acted superior and were thus often considered troublemakers. Although not explicitly, Aa Gym himself seemed to confirm this when telling me that such distrust "might be related to my past." He often confesses his lack of Islamic authority either at public talks or personal encounters. For example, when Aa Gym and I were having a conversation in the mosque and a follower approached him to ask that Aa Gym wish him good luck, Aa Gym told the follower: "Unlucky you are to attend Daarut Tauhid, a pesantren led by an unqualified leader like me." Thus, Aa Gym sees the negative response as partly arising from his own weaknesses.

Aa Gym also sees these negative responses as a predictable form of tension that his rapid emergence as a *kyai* would engender. The negative response is said to be most notable from the religious functionaries at the closest mosques. A functionary of the biggest mosque in KPAD complex, for example, felt overshadowed from his position since people now tended to pay more attention and thus respect to Aa Gym than to him. In facing this situation, Aa Gym tried to be wise in avoiding any conflict by making every attempt to maintain a good relationship. Aa Gym often praised him on many public occasions, acknowledging him as his religious teacher—as indeed he was. On many personal occasions, Aa Gym also tried to convince him that what he had been doing was his way of *ibadah*, purely for the sake of Allah. Aa Gym was eventually successful in convincing this functionary, who has since supported the development of Daarut Tauhid.

Pesantren Daarut Tauhid continues to grow amazingly, enjoying a profound support from Muslims locally and from a wider area. Its current form is only a strand of its continuum of rapid change. This portrait of the pesantren might be considerably different from that in the near future. Yet, regardless of this probable change, the nature of the relationships between the *kyai* and his followers will certainly shape these changes. Therefore, I would like to construct in the following chapter the pattern of these relationships. In so doing it is of course necessary to depict first the nature of both the leader and his followers.

ENDNOTES

[1] *Aa* is a Sundanese term used intimately to address a respectable, usually young, man or boy of an honourable family. When calling or naming the person, the Sundanese usually add the word before, often shortening, the actual name. Gymnastiar is therefore respectfully called *Aa Gym*, the second word standing for Gymnastiar.

[2] *Teh* is Aa Gym's intimate word to call his mother. It is, as a matter of fact, unusual to call one's own mother by the word *Teh* because it is actually a Sundanese word commonly used in calling any respectably elder woman other than one's mother. This misusage might be due to the influence of the surrounding people who call Aa Gym's mother by this word. And such due-to-the-surrounding usage is not in fact uncommon in Sundanese society.

[3] It is common in Bandung, and all over Indonesia, that for the *SIPENMARU*, SMA-graduates tend to do the so-called *BIMBEL* (*Bimbingan Belajar*, an intensive short-course) which focuses heavily on the strategy for facing *SIPENMARU*. Aa Gym, however, did not attend this course and did his own study instead.

[4] Note that Arabic-origin Indonesian words *shalat* and *do'a* are translated in English dictionaries equally as 'prayer.' The verb 'to pray' means either *melakukan shalat/sembahyang* or *berdo'a*.

[5] As is widely known, there are only five obligatory *shalat* each day. These are *shalat shubuh* (the dawn prayer), *shalat dhuhur* (the noon prayer), *shalat ashar* (the afternoon prayer), *shalat maghrib* (the sunset prayer), and *shalat isya* (the evening prayer).

[6] The period before the coming of Islam in Arabia is believed by Muslims to be the *masa jahiliyah* (period of ignorance) because of the common practices that were considered irreligious.

[7] The Prophet Muhammad said: "The ulamas are the heirs of the Prophets."

[8] It is worth noting that "gaining" the *lailatul qodar* has been the dream of many, if not all, Muslims. In the world very few Muslims gain *lailatul qodar* each year so that it is very special and valuable opportunity.

[9] The history of Java is rich with this kind of story. For example, Prabu Brawijaya, the last ruler of Majapahit, later well-known as Pandhanarang, devoted the last dozen years of his life to praying and meditating, before he emerged as a Javano-Islamic figure known as Sunan Tembayad (Fox 1991; Jamhari 1995; Pemberton 1994:279).

[10] This belief in *hikmah* and *baraka* disseminated through Agung is related to the Islamic ethic of facing illness. Illness is conceived of as either a divine "test" to the quality of the faith of a sinless Muslim or a divine "warning" to a sinful one. In either case, illness is a means by which Allah may either upgrade the quality of the faith or forgive the sins of any ill-suffering Muslim provided he is *sabar* (patient) enough in facing the illness, in such a way that he becomes more pious instead of *ngarasula* (grumbling and blaming) Allah. Agung was viewed as very *sabar* in facing his paralysis so that, being free from any sin, he had a special position in the "eye" of the Almighty Allah. In such a position, Agung was considered appropriate to be the passive medium for both generating *hikmah* and transmitting *baraka*.

[11] The Sundanese text on the picture reads: Aa Gym and his followers often wear a distinctive form of dress, yet he obliges neither himself nor his followers to wear it. They talk little but work hard. Aa Gym does everything without any sense of exaggeration. H. ABDULLAH GYMNASTIAR WAS VISITED BY THE PROPHET IN DREAMS SO THAT HE FOUNDED THE *BENGKEL AKHLAQ* DAARUT TAUHID.

[12] The ONH (*Ongkos Naik Haji*, costs for undertaking the *hajj*) for Indonesian Muslims was by 1987 five millions rupiah and is now seven millions rupiah for each individual. This is an all-inclusive cost that covers the cost of administrative management, transportation, accommodation, and catering in Mecca and Madina.

[13] *Haji* is a Sundanese, even more widely Indonesian, title given to any Muslim who has done the *hajj* to Mecca. It is commonly abbreviated as the initial H, standing for *haji*. When, say, Ahmad has done the *hajj*, his full name would be H. Ahmad.

[14] *Miqat* is the starting point where pilgrims formally start their *hajj* rituals. It is symbolised by declaring *niat* (intention), putting on specific *hajj* clothing, and performing optional *shalat*.

[15] Note that the *niat* to perform *hajj* itself is called *niat ihram* (intention of forbidding), originally meaning that a pilgrim has to intend leaving behind any preconditionally forbidden acts during the *hajj*, such as husband-wife intercourse.

[16] An essential cycle of *shalat* ritual consists of bows and prostrations performed a prescribed number of times.

[17] The phrases are "*Labbaika Allohumma Labbaik. La Syariika Laka Labbaik*" meaning "At Thy service, O Allah. No ally to You and, again, at Thy service O Allah."

[18] Aa Gym's views on the *hajj* were summarised from Qolbun Salim No. 010/Thn II. 28 May 1993.

[19] As a matter of fact, changing one's name after making the *hajj* had been the tradition of Indonesian pilgrims but it is less common now.

[20] I was told by his father that the name "Gymnastiar" is partly derived from ASEAN GAME (Asia's Olimpic) since Aa Gym was born at the time that ASEAN GAMES were on going.

[21] The word *ulama* was the very word that Aa Gym used at the time. In fact, Arabic *ulama* is the plural form of *'alim* so that the article *an* there does not in fact agree with the word. It is however common in Indonesia to apply the word *ulama* as either plural or singular. In this case, the word *ulama* has become Indonesian.

[22] See Mastuhu (1994:19) for further discussion of this specification of the pesantren tradition.

[23] Since *ajudan* is in fact an ABRI-term, one might well be struck how it was so readily taken up the tradition of Daarut Tauhid. This will be discussed when I deal with the structure of interrelationships within Daarut Tauhid in Chapter Four.

[24] An Arabic-origin phrase, *shilaturrahmi* means the ties of familial relationship including both consanguinial relatives and affinal families. In a wider sense, the phrase has been conceived of to mean bonds of Muslim brotherhood in the light that Muslims, anywhere of the world, are of one big family. In its widest understanding, the phrase has been understood to mean bonds of any friendship, thus including harmonious relationships even with non-Muslims. This term is used by Aa Gym in this widest meaning and so it has been practically applied at Daarut Tauhid.

[25] The *badan wakaf* (the donation board) was part of the old pesantren tradition, the *yayasan* reflects a modern way of social organising, recently adopted by many pesantren. In practice, both the *badan wakaf* and the *yayasan* play a more or less similar role in the pesantren tradition.

Chapter 3: The Leader, the Followers, and the Pattern of Relationships

Chapter Two has traced the process by which the pesantren Daarut Tauhid initially grew. We have seen that the foundation of the pesantren Daarut Tauhid was not the result of a solo effort by either its leader, Aa Gym, or his followers, but the fruit of their relatively equal contributions. Both were equally important driving forces in the foundation of the pesantren, although they would not explicitly claim this because, to them, it was nothing but the implementation of the will of Allah.

In this chapter, I will examine certain aspects of the relations between the leader and his followers. I shall in the first place examine the leader in terms of his personal qualities and popularity. The miraculous power of Aa Gym, as an important part of social recognition, is also raised here. I will then examine the followers in terms of their number, diversity, identity, and reasons for devotion before I attempt to construct the interrelationships between the leader and his followers; cognitive-rational, affective-emotional, and entrepreneurial.

3.1 The Leader: Personal Qualities and Popularity

Aa Gym, as the leader of the pesantren Daarut Tauhid, is both a *kyai* and a manager. On the one hand, he is the *kyai* of the pesantren in relation to its religious activities and, on the other hand, he is the manager of it in relation to its thirteen entrepreneurial activities. His role as both a *kyai* and manager is not only made possible but also plausible by his personal qualities. It is these qualities which I will now examine.

While Geertz oversimplifies the term *kyai* as roughly comparable to the Middle Eastern *ulama* (1960:134), I tend to follow Dhofier (1980:68), who describes it as "a title for Muslim scholars in Java who generally lead pesantren institutions."[1] Inherent attributes of a *kyai* are Islamic scholarship and pesantren leadership. Other related attributes supposedly possessed by a *kyai* include *ahli ibadah* (totally devout), and *muballigh* (Islamic preacher). They may also act as a kind of consultant on religious matters. These ideal attributes of the *kyai* will serve as important elements in discussing the personal qualities and popularity of Aa Gym.

Aa Gym became a *kyai* without following the stages through which Javanese *kyai* usually progress. In describing the usual progression, Dhofier (1980:72-73) writes:

Photograph 6 Aa Gym: a young *kyai* with extraordinary qualities though without pesantren education.

> To become a *kyai*, a novice…is usually a close relative of a *kyai*. After completing his studies at various pesantren, the older *kyai* train him to establish his own pesantren. Sometimes, the older *kyai* leads and finances the new project… [Then] the old *kyai* will find him a spouse…from the place where the young *kyai* [is] to develop [his] new pesantren.

As was made clear in the previous chapter, Aa Gym is not a relative of any *kyai* but is instead from an army-family.[2] He did not attend any pesantren in the usual way, which would involve living in and studying there for years, but simply visited a number of *kyai* for a few hours. He was not a wanderer who sought Islamic knowledge from a number of pesantren over a period of several years, as is usually the case with the *kyai* of nearly all pesantren (Bailey 1986:197; Dhofier 1982:24; Pranowo 1991b:41-42; Zulkifli 1994:63,87). Nor did any established *kyai* "intervene" in the matters of Daarut Tauhid's finances or Aa Gym's spouse. The question is, then, why he has become and has been called by the people a *kyai*?

Aa Gym is considered to be an *ulama*, a prerequisite for being a *kyai*. Since *ulama* means "learned Muslim scholar", one might well wonder how one can become an *ulama* without ever receiving adequate Islamic-oriented education, such as would be acquired in a pesantren.

Although without adequate pesantren experience, Aa Gym has his own ways of acquiring Islamic knowledge. First, he exercises the tradition of *shilaturrahmi* (described in the previous chapter) as a means of improving his Islamic-knowledge. Second, he reads large numbers of Islamic reference materials. His living room is filled with a huge number of Islamic books and reference materials. After telling me that even his bedroom walls are covered with various books (Islamic and general), Aa Gym said:

> I will always make the effort to seek wider knowledge. But notwithstanding this, there is "other knowledge" which is unconsciously [divinely?] transmitted to support my *dakwah* (proselytization) activities. I actually am reluctant to tell anyone about this kind of knowledge transmission to which I have access. All I can say is what has been the fact that the knowledge I gain is usually much more than the time I can spend to read. This is in no way a rational matter and should actually be off the record. I can not explain to you any further. It was my wife, in fact, who told me this phenomenon because she knows well how much time I spend in reading and other ways of seeking knowledge.

This phenomenon reminds us of the notion of *ilmu ladunni* (bestowed knowledge) that has its origins in Sufistic tradition and often colours the pesantren tradition. Of the former tradition, Trimingham (1971:304) notes that *al-'ilm al-ladunni* (Sundanese, *ilmu laduni*) is knowledge that comes from Allah directly into the hearts of saints.[3] Of the latter, Dhofier (1980:94-5) records it as Islamic knowledge mastered without study which, instead, comes directly from Allah as the fruit of *ilham* (personal inspiration). Indeed, it has been said that Aa Gym gains knowledge partly in the form of *ilham*, believed to be from Allah.

This leads to the speculation about the best way and time to gain *ilmu laduni*. His followers believe that Aa Gym has a special status which has led to tremendous increases in his Islamic knowledge without the usual ways of acquisition. They are also obsessed in achieving this kind of Allah-bestowed knowledge since they believe that all Muslims have the chance to gain it provided they are close enough to Allah. The following *do'a* (prayer) is thus commonly said at Daarut Tauhid:

Allaahumma zidnii	O my Lord, increase in me
ilman ladduuniyya	ilmu laduni
wa fahman waasi'a	and comprehensive understanding.
Ya kaasyifa al-musykilah	O Allah, who is able to unveil any abtruse subject,
iksyif'an wujuuhi	show [knowledge] behind the surface
hadzihi al-ma'aani	of these concrete things
hattaa athla'a	so that I can know [what is behind the scene].[a]

[a] All *santri* can say this particular *do'a* by heart.

The most probable moment for Aa Gym to receive the divine *ilham* is during his reflective meditation periods. Since the *i'tikaf* experience in 1987, such reflection has become one of his routine activities. It is done mainly at night following the performance of *shalat tahajjud* (optional night prayer). It is also said that Aa Gym is usually supplied with *ilham* each time he needs instruction in order to advise others. People around him believe that he is being guided by Allah, via *ilham*, each time he delivers a public *pengajian*. That is why, a follower told me, Aa Gym never makes any preparations before the *pengajian*.

According to Aa Gym, acquiring *ilmu ladunni* is very simple. The key to it is the readiness of human beings to make themselves worthy of gaining it, by having the right condition of heart and mind. For this, he provides us with an analogy:

> Let me show you an analogy of a glass to portray this kind of knowledge acquisition. A glass, anytime it catches light, will look bright inside and will illuminate its surroundings, providing the glass is *bening* (clear) and clean and the water in it is *bening* as well. So, whenever we try to be pure—I say *try* because I do not claim that I am pure already—we will

have good feelings. Everything we see, hear, read, and feel will become useful sources of knowledge. So, all the time we undergo an extraordinary acceleration of knowledge.

Thus, *ilmu ladunni* can be bestowed by Allah on those Muslims with purity of heart and mind, a quality that makes one close enough to Allah in such a way that Allah is pleased to bestow on him/her certain knowledge beyond the conventional ways of learning. This is not, however, to say that *ilmu laduni* requires no way of knowledge acquisition. A *santri* said that such self-purification to get close to Allah involves a good deal of endeavour.[4]

Through these three ways of acquiring knowledge: visiting leading *kyai*; reading various sources; and acquiring *ilmu ladunni*, Aa Gym has appeared to his followers as an *ulama*. However, I should note Aa Gym's definition of *ulama*, which is slightly different from the common one. In common usage, *ulama* are those Muslim scholars who command advanced knowledge in Islamic matters. To Aa Gym, mastering a wide range of advanced Islamic knowledge is not the main point of being an *ulama*:

> Nowadays, the word *ulama* is commonly understood to refer only to those Muslim scholars of religious matters (*faqih*), whereas in the past it included those Muslim mathematicians, medical experts, economists, and other experts on general matters. Muslim people today tend to trivialise these latter scholars by not regarding them as *ulama*. To me, they are also *ulama* as long as their field of study can facilitate their Allah-fearing and consequent closeness to Him (QS. 35:28). One whose profession is only *tukang sablon* (silk-screening service), for example, may look like an *ulama* in the eyes of Allah as long as his professional work makes him close to Him; while his hands are busy working, his heart and tongue are busy doing *dzikir* remembering Allah and, in the meantime, he is thoroughly convinced that Allah is watching his every movement. He thus always tries to do his best in order to satisfy both Allah and his customers. If, say, the customer is thereby induced to follow his religious style of life, this *tukang sablon* has surely performed the function of *ulama*; that is, to be a medium of others' *keselamatan* (salvation) here in the world and the hereafter.[5]

Thus, to Aa Gym, the main point of *ulama* is not knowledge *per se* but how much it facilitates fear and closeness to Allah and how much it is exercised as a means of spreading the blessings of Allah. The kind of the knowledge possessed, whether religious or not, and its depth are not the question. The emphasis is on its impact on an individual's relationship with Allah.

One might well assume that Aa Gym's definition of the meaning of *ulama* seems to be intended to fit with his personal conditions. The elimination of the central importance of high Islamic knowledge and the inclusion of general, non-religious knowledge in defining *ulama* clearly fits Aa Gym's own situation. However correct this assumption may be, Aa Gym's definition of *ulama* has its justification in the Qur'an, as referred to by Aa Gym in the above quote.

Besides his "*ulama*ship," the second factor that facilitates Aa Gym's "*kyai*ship" is the fact that he is a convincing preacher. Apart from his regular public *pengajian* at Daarut Tauhid, he is extremely busy in fulfilling invitations to preach in many parts of Bandung and beyond. Almost no day passes without such engagements. Often he has to preach at three to four different places on a day, ranging from mosques to schools, offices, and universities. In other words, he preaches as often at schools, universities, and other places as at mosques. The underlying reason for Aa Gym's popularity as a preacher is clear from the followers' reasons for joining, below. The point to make here is that being a good preacher, who is a source of wisdom and advice on religious matters, is another essential attribute to Aa Gym being a respected *kyai*.

3.2 *Ma'unah*: the Miraculous Power of Aa Gym

When I first arrived at Daarut Tauhid, I was initially welcomed by Abdurrahman Yuri, who I later learned was Aa Gym's brother. He then told me that Aa Gym was delivering a talk somewhere in Bandung. In the middle of our talk, Aa Gym came in looking very tired. When I asked Yuri to let me see Aa Gym so that I could introduce myself and ask his permission to do fieldwork at Daarut Tauhid, Yuri replied: "Aa Gym looks very tired, I am afraid. He usually has a break at this time because he has to deliver the weekly *pengajian* here in less than an hour. In fact, he already knows of your intention to do fieldwork here. You may see him later on after the *pengajian*."

I do not know if Aa Gym really was aware of my intention to do fieldwork. This event illustrates how people surrounding Aa Gym believe in his extraordinary abilities. There are other examples of this kind of belief by the followers of Aa Gym.

Hakim is said to often see a shining light emanating from Aa Gym's *emunemunan* (crown of the head) while he is delivering religious talks. At other times, he sees a similar light shining from the roof of Aa Gym's house. Sometimes, when he sees this light, Hakim calls upon others to share what he is seeing: "Have a look there at Aa Gym's house. There looks to be a brightly shining moon." Some of the other people could see what Hakim was witnessing, others could not. It is thought that whether or not one can see depends on one's spiritual intensity. Hakim is said to exercise so much *dzikir* (remembrance or recollection of Allah's name) that he can often see what others may not be able to. A disciple once told me, "*Hakim mah sae dzikirna* (Hakim is good at performing *dzikir*)."

Another follower also told me of his strange experiences concerning Aa Gym. One day he and his mosque-mates invited Aa Gym to give a *ceramah* at the mosque. When everything was finished and Aa Gym wanted to go home, the car which was to transport Aa Gym was not available. While the team nervously waited, Aa Gym calmly said: "Do not worry. The car is over there. Let us go." And the car was where he said it would be. This may be an example of what Aa Gym's mother once told me: "Aa Gym often *kengeng ilapat* (foresees with the inspiration of Allah) what will happen."

K. H. Khoer Affandi, Aa Gym's counsellor, has also had extraordinary experiences with Aa Gym. He was amazed by the fact that each time Aa Gym came to visit him, other people always arrived before Aa Gym. They usually came with food which K. H. Khoer Affandi then served to Aa Gym and his accompanying followers. Aa Gym's mother quoted K. H. Khoer Affandi, "When many people send food in the morning, *Si Aa* [Aa Gym] is coming." So, according to K. H. Khoer Affandi, Aa Gym always came with a visible *barakah*. This *barakah* came into being in an extraordinary way, typical of Aa Gym as a *kyai*.

On another occasion, K. H. Khoer Affandi was delivering a *ceramah* to a wedding party, when he suddenly felt like going home. He stopped the *ceramah* before the due time, saying: "There is a guest from Bandung at home. I have to go." When he arrived at home, Aa Gym was waiting for him and was about to leave for Bandung to give a *ceramah* there.

These miraculous events which surround Aa Gym are referred to by his followers as *ma'unah*, miraculous gifts bestowed by Allah on an *ulama* or a *kyai*. This reference to *ma'unah* is based on a differentiation of miraculous gifts possessed by Islamic specialists in accordance with their status. The miraculous gifts of a prophet are referred to as *mu'jizat*, those of a candidate to prophethood are *irhash*, those of a saint are *karamah*, those of an *ulama* or a *kyai* are *ma'unah*, and those of infidels are *istidraj*. (Compare Mastuhu 1990:89, Zulkifli 1994:76.) When Dhofier refers to the *kyai*'s miraculous acts as *karomah* (1980c:53), perhaps this is because Muslims tend to attribute to the *kyai* some characteristics of sainthood, since sainthood is an overwhelming aspect of the history and the present practice of Javanese Islam (Fox 1991).[6] This is noted by Prasojo (1974:41), who writes: "Almost all *kyai* and great *'ulama* are believed as [to be?] *wali* [saint] who possess *kramat* [original italics]."[7] For example, Pranowo (1991a:33, 1991b:52) observes that *kyai* mBah Mangli in Magelang, and Pak Muh, the vice-leader of Tegal Rejo Pesantren, Central Java, are believed by the villagers to be a *wali* with a "mysterious" daily life.

3.3 The Followers: Numbers, Diversity, and Identity

It is difficult to determine the precise number of the followers of Daarut Tauhid, partly because the numbers are so large, and partly because, so far, no census has been taken. However, during gatherings of the *pengajian*, they fill not only the double-storeyed mosque, which has a capacity of at least two thousand, but also flow onto the stairs, yard, and the street. This gathering, known as the *Taushiyah Penyejuk Hati*, is held twice on Sundays afternoons and Thursday evenings. It is the occasion for a large number of followers to come together and thus the best time to gauge the size of Daarut Tauhid's following. Here one can see over two thousand people.

Photograph 7 The mosque was fully filled.

The audience flowed out onto the stairs and the yard.

One can also see the number of followers on other occasions: at the women's *pengajian* on Wednesdays and Saturdays; the study of classical Islamic texts held on Mondays, Tuesdays, and Wednesdays; and at religious workshops and courses held at Daarut Tauhid. The number of people attending these occasions ranges from at least two hundred to perhaps a thousand. Thus, as reported by *Mangle* (December 1993) and *Tempo* (April 1993), the number of Muslims attending Daarut Tauhid activities may reach three thousand.

This does not include Aa Gym's audiences at his frequent *pengajian* outside Daarut Tauhid. These audience, the great majority of whom are also to a certain extent loyal to Daarut Tauhid, are of course much more difficult to measure. Furthermore, Aa Gym is said to have some followers in other cities of Indonesia such as Jakarta, Semarang, and Denpasar and even abroad, such as in Singapore, Mecca, America, and Australia.

The vast majority of these followers are in their teens and twenties. I would estimate that the young comprise no less than 95 percent of the followers. There are even children of primary school age. Only rarely did I come across followers above forty years of age. In regard to gender, there are slightly more female followers than male. Based on the amount of space occupied at the gatherings, females appear to make up 60 percent of the followers.

Followers can be classified as either student or non-student. Given the youthfulness of the Daarut Tauhid membership, followers are predominantly students. These followers mainly attend either secondary or tertiary educational institutions. There appears to be relatively equal numbers of each. Put another way, there are more or less as many SMP and SMA students as university students. The latter are mostly undergraduate students of IKIP, Unpad, ITB, Unisba, and other surrounding universities, although there is also a significant number of postgraduate students. I recognised at least nine postgraduate student followers, although I suspect there are many others of whom I was not aware.

Apart from this predominance of student followers, there is a significant number of non-student followers. These range from public servants, merchants, workers and entrepreneurs to *beca* (pedicab) drivers and unemployed youths. As an example, *Kasoem Optical*, a famous optical dispensary in Bandung, regularly sends its workers to attend Daarut Tauhid's *pengajian* as a form of mental, in this case religious, training. The owner of *Kasoem Optical* finds it useful in motivating the workers and in fostering ethical behaviour. The owner himself regularly attends the *pengajian*.

The followers fall into two broad categories: *jema'ah* and *santri*. The former category, which represents the majority of followers, refers to those who do not stay at the Daarut Tauhid complex but still join in nearly all of its activities. The latter, the *santri*, refers to those followers who either stay at the Daarut Tauhid complex or work for the Daarut Tauhid, so that without staying there they spend almost all their time there.

There are three kinds of *santri* at Daarut Tauhid. The first is referred to as *santri mukim*, those who devote their time to the study of Islamic knowledge. They are thus like the santri of various pesantren throughout Indonesia, as noted by Dhofier (1980:61–62). This group is distinguished at Daarut Tauhid from the second type, *santri mahasiswa*. As the term suggests, they are university students who help Aa Gym manage and develop the pesantren Daarut Tauhid. This group originated among those people who were involved in the KMIW.[8] It is, I think, for this reason that this group is classified differently. This group could also be referred to as *santri pengurus* (managing santri), as it is in the pesantren tradition (see Geertz 1960:235–236). The third kind of the santri is called *santri karyawan* and refers to those santri who work for Daarut Tauhid's entrepreneurial activities.

While working, they have certain times in which to perform specific rituals in order to upgrade their spirituality.

Photograph 8 The santri having dinner together.

3.4 The Followers: Reasons for Joining

Notwithstanding that in some cases religious affiliation may be the result of political interest or social pressure, the main reason for people's participation in religious activities is that they believe the spiritual benefits they may obtain are necessary for their life in this world and in the next.[9] This appears to be the case with Muslims who join Daarut Tauhid. The usual reason for followers joining Daarut Tauhid is to improve their spirituality as a means by which they can cope with personal and social problems.

One of the spiritual benefits enjoyed by Daarut Tauhid's followers is the reinforcement of Islamic morality. As part of the Daarut Tauhid's "trademark," the *Bengkel Akhlaq* (Workshop of Morality), the followers gain a sort of religious energy and a set of ethical codes which help to order their lives. They feel easy and harmonious living in this world with the conviction of gaining salvation hereafter.

One might well ask why it is Daarut Tauhid that these people join, and not some other Islamic centres? After all, there are a great number of alternative Islamic centres which provide numerous Islamic activities for the Muslims of Bandung. Yet these attract only a few participants and these followers are generally elderly. What are the reasons why people prefer to join Daarut Tauhid?

Firstly, most followers claim that they gain what they call *ketenangan batin* (inner peace). Many frankly acknowledged their previous inner instability due to their *akhlaq jelek* (irreligious manners). During a time of uncertainty, they needed religious guidance, and, according to them, they found what they needed at Daarut Tauhid, and not anywhere else. According to one SMA-follower who had been a member for about a year:

> Praise absolutely be to Allah who has by his might provided us with Daarut Tauhid, a locus of restless people looking for Allah's *kurnia* (blessing). Before joining Daarut Tauhid and Aa Gym in particular, my *akhlaq* was far worse than it is today. By the will of Allah, I have been feeling *sejuk hati* (inner comfort). For example, I am now certain of how to cope with anxiety, because I know whom to rely upon, and other things that make our problems easy to overcome.

With a similar tone, another statement was made by another follower, who is a worker for a private company:

> I dropped out of SMP due to my involvement in *hura-hura remaja* (juvenile delinquency). I joined Daarut Tauhid because I wanted to replace the immoral part of my life with Islamic morality. And it works. I am now fully conscious of all the sins I committed before. I do my best in asking Allah's forgiveness by, for example, doing good deeds in the world.

These two similar statements show Daarut Tauhid's efficacy in carrying out its mission. The primary mission of Daarut Tauhid as a *Bengkel Akhlaq* is to provide moral, religious ways in which to make one's life both orderly and stable, as Luthfi, a Daarut Tauhid officer, once told me. How this works will be discussed in Chapter Five.

Secondly, Aa Gym is an exemplary figure at a time when there is a perceived shortage of such individuals in the Muslim world who are relevant to the young. Moreover, Aa Gym is a young man with a high personal degree of religious piety. This serves as another factor which draws the attention of young people. Aa Gym suggested this as a possible factor when I asked his opinion on why young Muslims have been gathering around him. "Perhaps," he said, "it is simply because I am of their age, so they probably consider me as a fellow."

However, my interviews with most followers reveal something more than a similarity of ages as a reason for following him. A 20 years-old female *santri* said:

> Aa Gym functions as a good "father" for all. He can help us become mature by making our lives meaningful. His advice always facilitates us to change all the time, holding that a minute without change is a disadvantage. He is a living example of applied Islamic morality such as

modesty, sincerity, and discipline. We pay respect to him for his modesty. He never claims the status of a teacher for himself. He seems to feel as though he is also a *santri* without any tendency to be superior. Instead, he often claims that he is not so perfect a Muslim. These features of his make me salute him and I hope Allah maintains Aa Gym's *istiqomah* (consistency) in being so.

The young Aa Gym is perceived by this follower as a "father" who guides the ordering of her life by means of both oral instructions and behavioural examples.

Another aspect of Aa Gym's exemplary qualities is leadership. Many followers stressed this aspect.

Aa Gym is the best motivator and the most disciplined leader I have ever met, who works for the sake of his *ummat*, often neglecting himself.

Aa Gym is both authoritative and fully self-reliant. Besides, he is also effective in motivating his followers towards disciplined worship and good deeds.

As a leader, Aa Gym is also admired for giving precedence to the *ummat* (Muslim community). An SMA-student follower, for instance, said: "Aa Gym pays more attention towards his *ummat* than towards himself. In other words, his concern with *ummat* has priority over his personal interests."

Many followers are attracted by Aa Gym's personal charisma. A male follower, who is a worker at a private company, told me the experience of his first encounter with Aa Gym:

I spontaneously "fell in love" on first contact with Aa Gym. When his sharp eyes gazed into mine I could not make eye contact (*tak sanggup menatapnya*), but it really made my heart *sejuk* (comfortable). I do not understand why.

The third reason why followers join is that they enjoy the wisdom which Aa Gym provides through his *pengajian*, known as *Taushiyah Penyejuk Hati* (Comforting Religious Advice). According to them, Aa Gym's advice in the *pengajian* is different from that of any other *kyai* or Islamic *muballigh* (preachers). A follower pointed to this difference saying: "From the *pengajian* Aa Gym delivers, I feel that Allah is very close to me, so that I gain a sort of *kedamaian hati* (inner peace)." This satisfaction is confirmed by the following statement of an SMA-student:

While I see no concluding word to express my satisfaction generated from listening to Aa Gym's *pengajian*, I can just say that its themes and his style of wording *begitu menyentuh hati* (touch my deepest feelings). The first time I heard Aa Gym's voice was on Madina radio. I instantly "felt in love" and have since come to Daarut Tauhid to attend the *pengajian*.

These quotes demonstrate the effectiveness of Aa Gym's words in promoting a religious sense in listeners' hearts and minds. Indeed, as will be discussed in Chapter Five, a *qolbun salim* (an orderly heart) is the primary target of Daarut Tauhid.

Another aspect of the *pengajian* that attracts followers is Aa Gym's persuasive quality. A female university student suggested that

> the way Aa Gym preaches does not sound *mendikte* (instructive). His *pengajian* is not delivered in a monotone because its themes are various and full of improvisations that are suitable to the current affairs of society.

This was confirmed by a high school student, who sees the effectiveness of Aa Gym's persuasion that considers the varying age levels of the audience. This female student said: "Aa Gym is very keen on choosing themes and ways of delivering for every different age group in the audience. Besides, his words are so practical in nature."

What is meant by 'practical' above is that what Aa Gym advises is easy to understand and is relevant to the practical interests of the listeners. Aa Gym often gives examples related and relevant to current affairs. Aa Gym's language in his public talks is also a familiar one to the listeners. A man, who is a worker at a private company, commented on the language of Aa Gym: "His *pengajian* is attractive because he speaks in *bahasa murah dan sederhana* (popular, vernacular language); the language of the younger generation that is easy to catch, yet is emotionally sensitive."

Given these advantages of Aa Gym's *pengajian*, the followers find it distinctive. A high school student thus said that

> Aa Gym is the first *muballigh* (preacher) I have ever met who gives so much useful advice. He is, to me, the only one who can change one's life towards that which is in line with Allah's blessing.

Many followers expressed views similar in meaning to the quote above. The quote thus reflects the general attitude of the followers towards the style of Aa Gym's *pengajian*. To miss out Aa Gym's *pengajian* is, in turn, felt by many followers as a big loss.

The fourth reason followers gave for joining is the effectiveness of Daarut Tauhid's rituals in generating followers' awareness of their sins and in convincing them of Allah's forgiveness of their sins. The main ritual in this regard is the *wirid dan do'a*,[10] which is held after every *pengajian*. Most of the followers find this ritual as indispensable as the *pengajian* itself.

> The words Aa Gym employs during the *wirid dan do'a* are almost always relevant to my circumstances. They bring to my memory all the sins I committed so that I cry regretting, repenting, and hoping for Allah's forgiveness.

This claim of a University student is confirmed by a high school student who finds that "the ritual lets me recall all the former *maksiat* (immoral manners) and *munkarat* (disavowals) I committed. I feel ashamed of myself before Allah because of breaking His law."

The key point of Daarut Tauhid's rituals is their effectiveness in raising its followers' awareness of their sinfulness. This can be further seen from the following experience of a follower.

> I feel ashamed of myself when I am involved in the *wirid dan do'a*. I feel as though I am *ditelanjangi* (exposed); that is I realise all my abundant sins and I feel I have nothing to be proud of in the face of Allah. I feel as if I understand Aa Gym's Arabic *do'a* whereas I do not speak Arabic at all.

Another key point of the rituals is their offer of a way out from sinfulness to purity. This inheres in the *do'a* said to Allah. The *do'a* certainly bear some hope for a better future. The distinctive feature in reciting the *do'a* is the fact that Aa Gym most frequently says the *do'a* in Indonesian. As an officer told me, this is the reason why the followers, nearly all of whom do not speak Arabic, understand the *do'a* and are thus completely involved in the ritual. Otherwise, they could not follow the *do'a* and are thus less involved in it and gain little if anything from the ritual, something I have often witnessed in Muslim rituals elsewhere, whose language is commonly Arabic.

The fifth reason for joining is the harmonious combination at Daarut Tauhid between worldly and eschatological orientations. There is an equal emphasis at Daarut Tauhid on both spiritual and worldly activities. For example, they may have prayer sessions at one time, and go hiking and camping at another. Daarut Tauhid's recommendation to people to acquire as much money as possible while not forgetting to thank Allah, the ultimate source of wealth, is another example of this combination. In this way, Daarut Tauhid is therefore neither anti-wealth nor anti-modern styles of life. Being a pious Muslim does not mean being opposed to modern life but, on the contrary, the two are indispensable to each other. This combination[11] was summed up by a follower, a journalist in his early thirties, who said that "Aa Gym is a figure who is successful in combining *amal dhahir* (exoteric deed) and *amal batin* (esoteric deed)."

In addition to these five reasons, some followers say that Aa Gym's personal history resembles their own, in that Aa Gym previously had more or less similar experiences of juvenile delinquency as many of his followers had, or continue to have. As described earlier, it was not until 1987 that Aa Gym was drawn to a more rigorous practice of Islam. As he frequently discloses in his public *pengajian*, he had been less pious then and was often involved in irreligious behaviour although he still practised the obligatory *shalat*. Aa Gym's earlier experiences parallel those of the great majority of his followers. They thus have a sense of *senasib* (sharing the same fate), which I think is essential to Aa Gym's exemplary status. The follower is inspired by Aa Gym's example in escaping from juvenile delinquency into a more religious life.

These six characteristics of Daarut Tauhid are less likely to be found at other Islamic centres in Bandung, and that is why people join.

3.5 The Patterns of Relationship

Given the characteristics of leader and follower, the interrelationships between them are quite different to those of either *kyai-santri* relationships at other pesantren, or social relationships in general. In this section I will describe three typical relationships between leader and follower to be found at Daarut Tauhid.

The first I call the cognitive-rational relationship. By this I mean the relationship through which knowledge is transmitted in Daarut Tauhid. There are two kinds of knowledge transmission at Daarut Tauhid: formal and informal.

In the case of formal knowledge transmission, which is common to any teacher-student relationship, Aa Gym functions as the source of knowledge while the follower (the *jemaah* and the *santri*) acts as his students. Aa Gym's knowledge is transmitted at the twice-weekly *Taushiyah Penyejuk Hati*, the *taushiyah* following every congregational *shalat*, and various workshops and training courses.

In this formal relationship, the followers tend to play a passive role in that they just listen and then practise what they have learned. They believe that what Aa Gym says comes from Allah and is thus absolutely true. Although followers did raise questions during the *pengajian*, I never heard any question that put Aa Gym's preaching in doubt. Most, if not all, of the questions simply asked Aa Gym's advice on problems faced by followers. One woman asked, for example, how to cope with her anger towards her unfaithful boyfriend while Islam, as Aa Gym often preaches, teaches Muslims not to hate anyone.

Informal knowledge transmission is more typical than formal transmission of knowledge. Here, the process of knowledge transmission is viewed as timeless, and both the Aa Gym and the follower become at once the "teacher" and the "student." Concerning this, Aa Gym said:

> In this system, all of us play the role of the teacher and the student. There is no time without learning. I learn as many lessons from others as they from me. Similarly, the *santri* here always try to learn from each

other and from the system itself. Thus the learning process happens all the time.

Not all followers have access to the process of informal transmission of knowledge because not all of them have personal relationships with Aa Gym. This informal relationship happens exclusively with *santri* followers, because they live in or work for Daarut Tauhid. Thus only they have the relatively constant, close contact with Aa Gym necessary to evolve personal relationships. *Jemaah* followers are less likely to have this relationship with Aa Gym, because they only visit Daarut Tauhid either twice weekly, to attend the *pengajian*, or daily, to attend the *pengajian* and the study of classical Islamic texts, or periodically to carry out workshops and retreats.

The second interrelationship within Daarut Tauhid is what I would call the affective-emotional relationship. In discussing this, three notions are relevant: charisma, *barakah*, and fellowship.

As is almost always the case with local grass-roots leaders, such as the Javanese *kyai*, Aa Gym is highly charismatic. The dreams involving the Prophet Muhammad, the miraculous power of *ma'unah*, and his extraordinary ability to gain the *ilmu laduni* provide the core of his charisma. This is compounded by his managerial leadership and religious piety. Having those charismatic qualities allows Aa Gym to be conceived of as a channel for *barakah* (divine blessing), not the other way around, as Dhofier (1980c:53) suggests: "…being a source of *barakah* allow[s] *kyai* to develop charismatic leadership."

The relationship between Aa Gym and his followers is therefore similar to that between the *murshid* and the *murid* of the Sufistic traditions or between the holy men and the laity among tribal traditions. Besides being the source of religious knowledge and advice, Aa Gym is viewed by his followers as a channel of *barakah*. [Note that he is a "channel", rather than a "source" of *barakah* (see again Dhofier above), since, for them, only Allah can be the source of divine blessings, humans can only be a channel.] Followers kissing his hand, in the hope of receiving *barakah*, was a phenomenon I witnessed either following every *pengajian* or on personal encounters. Aa Gym once told his audience, in which I was a member, the same phenomenon occurred in Singapore after he delivered a *pengajian* there.

The notion of *barakah* also allows followers to ask Aa Gym for specific *do'a*, for it is believed that offering a *do'a* to Allah through Aa Gym is most likely, if not definitely, to be attended to by Allah. This is supported by the well-known recommendation of K. H. Khoer Affandi: "Go to Aa Gym as often as you can because I find his *do'a* to Allah highly attended."

This notion of *barakah* seems to be often spoken of by Aa Gym. That Aa Gym publicly told his audience about his experience in Singapore suggests this inclination to highlight *barakah*. He also claimed that his extensive knowledge of Islam was partly gained via the *barakah* generated from his deep respect for the *ulama*, particularly those who personally guide him, such as K. H. Khoer Affandi. He seemed to suggest that his acquisition of *ilmu ladunni* is in part a result of *barakah*. At a *pengajian* I attended, he told the audience a story exemplifying this aspect of *barakah*.

> A *santri*, it was said, of a great *kyai* used to serve and help the *kyai*. He went wherever the *kyai* went, helping him with everything such as bringing the *kyai*'s bag. He also washed his clothes and other items such as shoes and thongs. In short, he acted as the servant of the *kyai* instead of studying as a santri. This was all he did during his stay at the *kyai*'s pesantren. After several years the *kyai* asked the servant *santri* to leave the pesantren and found a pesantren of his own. When the *santri*, being aware that he had never studied and thus had no competent knowledge, did not believe him and told the *kyai* that it was impossible, the *kyai* replied: "Just go and rely upon Allah. I am convinced you have much Islamic knowledge to teach."

The knowledge of this santri is held to be Allah-given and generated from *barakah* by serving the *kyai*.

Needless to say, this kind of story has a considerable impact, intended or not, on his followers' attitudes towards him. This leads an observer to judge that some followers demonstrate a sort of *kultus individu* (the cult of the individual) towards Aa Gym (Karim 1993:63). While this judgement may be true to a certain extent, any cult of the individual tends to be the result of the follower's awe at the personal qualities of Aa Gym, and it is actually kept to a minimum both by the modesty of Aa Gym and by the friendly relations he promotes with his followers.

The third relationship I want to mention is therefore that of fellowship. Aa Gym tends to view his followers, particularly those of the *santri* category, as his colleagues in developing the pesantren and in orienting the *jemaah* and Muslims at large. They work together on the basis of give and take. Interestingly, this fellowship does not minimise the follower's respect for Aa Gym, perhaps because of Aa Gym's aweinspiring personal qualities. There is thus a balance between the tendency to create a cult around the personality of Aa Gym and the relational intimacy he promotes. In this way, the intimate fellowship is part of Aa Gym's charisma. (Compare Guinness 1986:180-181.)

In order to promote this intimacy, Aa Gym appears to feel free doing things that other *kyai* never do. For example, he has his weekly turn at sweeping the pesantren environment. Note that Daarut Tauhid has also taken the initiative to perform *opsih* (clean up activities) in the area around its complex. Daarut Tauhid takes the initiative to place rubbish bins throughout the streets and to clean the streets daily. Aa Gym takes his turn at this every Friday. Another example is that Aa Gym himself once called *Adzan*, which other *kyai* never do, to mark *shalat maghrib* time. At that time, his followers, as well as myself, were breaking the fast since it was Ramadhan. After saying *Adzan*, he broke the fast with his followers, as though he were one of them. These examples illustrate the extent of fellowship relations.

Finally, there exists what can be termed an entrepreneurial relationship. As briefly mentioned earlier, Daarut Tauhid runs a number of businesses ranging from computer rental and selling handicrafts, to a mini-market and a mini-bank. The entrepreneurial relationship between pesantren Daarut Tauhid and its followers is vital to the economic endeavours of the pesantren.

Photograph 9 A number of followers having their picture taken together with their beloved and much admired *kyai* (holding the microphone): an intimate relationship as part of the charisma.

The followers, first of all, are the best clients of the pesantren's entrepreneurial activities. They are the best customers of Daarut Tauhid's mini-market, which provides daily needs and services, as are they of the rental services provided by the pesantren, such as sound systems, transportation, and so on. They are also the potential *nasabah* (customers) for Daarut Tauhid's mini-bank, *Data Baitut Tamwil*.[12] It was only founded in June 1994 and, within six months of development, it had gained national recognition as the best mini-bank run by a pesantren. Its fast growth owes much to the followers' perception: that taking part in it is, besides a way of saving, a form of charity because Daarut Tauhid promises to spend the profit mainly in helping poor people develop ways of earning income, and that helping the mini-bank grow is a communal effort in developing the Muslim community. This perception applies to other aspects of Daarut Tauhid's economic ventures. Daarut Tauhid thus provides, and benefits from, an economic engagement with its followers that has religious meaning, an added value to other, more purely secular, economic activities.

Seen from another angle of economics, the followers function for Daarut Tauhid as a very effective instrument of advertisement. When returning home, followers bring with them oral, sometimes printed, information about what Daarut Tauhid has to offer and what is going on there. In fact, the distribution of information by followers on behalf of the pesantren applies to all sorts of activities of Daarut Tauhid. For example, the massive attendance at *pengajian* and short-term workshops and training courses also owes much to these distribution activities. The dissemination of information by the followers becomes an information network that spreads wider and wider in accordance with the increasing number of followers.

Finally, the followers are deeply concerned contributors of both ideas and critiques on the development of Daarut Tauhid. Suggestion boxes by which they can air their thoughts have been provided. Aa Gym said that Daarut Tauhid is a Muslim owned centre, and that they are all involved in making it better.

ENDNOTES

[1] However, when I mention *kyai* I will not restrict myself only to 'traditionalist *ulama*' as Dhofier did, because not all *kyai* belong to a traditionalist tradition, as, for example, is the case with Aa Gym himself.

[2] Horikoshi records that a number of the great *kyai* in Cipari, West Java, were the descendants of *Kyai* Zainal Abidin (1976:186-191). Bailey notes six *kyai* in Nangoh, West Java, were the offspring of *Kyai* Munasan (1986:170-171). And Dhofier found thirty great *kyai* throughout Java were the offspring of *Kyai* Sihah (1982:63-65).

[3] William Chittick, in his *Ibn al-'Arabi's Metaphysics of Imagination: The Sufi Path of Knowledge* (1989), offers a long description on this kind of Allah-given knowledge as an important part of the Sufi tradition.

[4] Dhofier (1980:95n) emphasises the role of parents in producing children with the ability of acquiring *ilmu laduni*. For this, a Sundanese *kyai*, Dhofier writes, told him eight practices and rituals the parents are to perform: "(a) during pregnancy, the parents must always be in harmony with each other...they are not allowed to quarrel,...; (b) immediately after birth *adhan* and *iqomah*...rituals must be offered; (c) honey must be the first food given to the baby, and before the honey is given, the feeder must pronounce *Bismillah al-rahman al-rahim*... 786 times; (d) the mother must not suckle the baby while she is angry; (e) as soon as the child reaches three years of age he must be taught tawhid; (f) when he is five years old, he must be taught to read the Qur'an and must learn the obligatory rituals; (g) when he reaches adulthood, he must practise *qanaah* (asceticism) such as fasting; and (h) the parents and the child should always *prihatin* (practice of an austere life)."

When I asked Aa Gym's parents whether they did these practices, they answered that they were ignorant of that kind of "recipe" for having a child with *ilmu laduni*. Aa Gym's mother just told me that indeed she used to practise *qanaah* and *prihatin* before marriage. What she did after marriage and during her pregnancy with Aa Gym was simply to practise Islam as properly as she could and to pray to Allah to have *shaleh* (pious) children.

[5] Qolbun Salim No. 088, Thn. III, 1995, p. 2.

⁶ *Wali* (saints) are believed to be the bringers of Islam to Indonesia (Geertz 1960:39). Some traditions argue that there were thousands of pious people, considered to be *wali*, who spread Islam in Java (Jamhari 1995:15). The most famous among them were *walisanga*, the Nine Saints. See Fox (1991) for further elaboration on the significance of these *wali* and the controversy about their existence.

⁷ The various transliteration of *karamah, karomah, kramat*, and *karama* all come from the same Arabic root. This variation does not imply any difference in meaning.

⁸ KMIW stands for *Keluarga Mahasiswa Islam Wiraswasta* (Entrepreneurial Group of Muslim Students). It was the embryo for Daarut Tauhid before it was set up as a pesantren in 1990. See Chapter Two on the foundation of Daarut Tauhid.

⁹ Socio-political motivation is frequently of importance when we are speaking of conversion or affiliation to a religion. See, for instance, Hefner's "Of Faith and Commitment: Christian Conversion in Muslim Java" in *Conversion to Christianity* edited by Hefner (1993:99–125).

¹⁰ The nature of this ritual is described in Chapter Five.

¹¹ A fuller description of this combination is given in the following chapter.

¹² *Data* stands for Daarut Tauhid, while *Baitut Tamwil* is an Arabic term for banking, literally meaning the store of wealth. *Data Baitut Tamwil* is Daarut Tauhid's bank that operates savings and loans, just like usual banks. However, it attempts to implement an Islamic banking system that is based on Islamic principles of cooperation. It offers, for example, an equal division of benefits, instead of offering interest that is considered to be forbidden *riba* (usury).

Chapter 4: Creative Expression Eschatological and Worldly Orientations

Characteristics of the leader, the follower, and their patterns of relationship as portrayed in the preceding chapter are given form by the distinctively creative expressions of Islam initiated by Aa Gym and further institutionalised in the life of Daarut Tauhid. As the adjective 'creative' implies, these expressions of Islam contain many things new to, or at least distinguishable from, local commonly-held understandings and practices of Islam. This is not to suggest that the Islam of Daarut Tauhid has been uprooted from the supposedly original Islam. It is rather a creative adaptation to current social demands.

The practice of Islam at Daarut Tauhid involves some novel combinations between Islamic orientations previously conceived of as being in opposition. This chapter will discuss the nature of such combinations with some comparisons to other practices of Islam and religions at large.

While many Muslims tend to practise Islam based on the prevailing natural-supernatural dichotomy,[1] those at Daarut Tauhid see no reason to separate the two. They instead view the two as different sides of the same religious coin and therefore as having to be practised together. Neglecting one of the two is as dangerous as ignoring the other. In other words, there must be a sort of delicate combination of the two. This principle is seen in the following aspects of Daarut Tauhidian Islamic practices.

4.1 The World and Beyond: A Balance

Features of life commonly viewed as worldly and frequently excluded from recent Islamic attention are paid as much attention by Daarut Tauhid as religious concerns. This orientation is clearly observable in both practical and conceptual levels at the pesantren. I shall portray this by describing first its religious and then its worldly practices and concepts.

As at other Islamic centres, Muslims at Daarut Tauhid are involved in both individual and congregational religious practices. *Shalat*, in its various forms and at various times, serves as the cardinal pillar for their spiritual activities. They perform the *shalat* congregationally and, more frequently, individually. It takes place at daytime and, more often, at night. It is generally done at the mosque and only rarely at home. There is almost always at least one person performing *shalat* at the mosque.

At nights, when surrounding houses are both dark and quiet, the Daarut Tauhid's mosque still looks alive, as though the santri are taking turns in performing rituals at the mosque. As a matter of fact, there are no strictly scheduled turns:

the performance of rituals relies on individual obligation. As part of its training, Daarut Tauhid requires santri to perform optional *shalat* every night, to record the performance by filling in a form, and then to report it to the supervisor who is none other than the *kyai*. This is said to be highly effective in internalising an individual sense of discipline.

Besides exercising *shalat*, they also practise *wirid, do'a*, and meditative reflection, such as *i'tikaf*. These are mainly done at night, although are sometimes performed during the day. As noted earlier, a profound significance in drawing followers has been attributed to these particular rituals, without which Daarut Tauhid would be unattractive as a religious routine. Needless to say, Daarut Tauhid also exercises the fulfilment of other pillars of Islam: *zakat* (alms), *shaum* (fasting), and *hajj* (pilgrimage to Mecca), all of which are commonly exercised by other Muslims through other Islamic centres. It is instead important to note that Daarut Tauhidians subscribe, in addition to obligatory rites, to many optional practices such as *shalat tahajjud* (overnight prayer), *shalat taubat* (repenting prayer), *shaum Senin-Kamis* (fasting on Mondays and Thursdays), *shadaqoh* (charity), and so on.[2]

The use of Islamic symbols also asserts the religious intensity of Muslims at Daarut Tauhid. Needless to say, the *kerudung* (female head-cover), the very noticeable identity of Muslim women, is commonly worn by Daarut Tauhid's female followers. Newcomers, who are not yet used to wearing it, usually need only a week or so before they are persuaded of its indispensability to Islam. In regard to the endless conflict between Muslims who view the *kerudung* as indispensable and those who see it as dispensable, Daarut Tauhid is definitely in the former camp. In practice, however, the decision as to whether or not it should be worn is left to individuals. Aa Gym's persuasive abilities on this point is best-illustrated by the following example.

> At a *pengajian* occasion I attended, a female follower raised a question with Aa Gym. Claiming that she was a newcomer at Daarut Tauhid pengajian, she frankly confessed to not wearing any *kerudung*. However, she declared her willingness to wear it in the near future, but could not imagine the responses to her new appearance with *kerudung*. She thus begged Aa Gym's advice on the matter. After emphasising that she had every right to wear it or not to wear it, Aa Gym said that covering one's *aurat* (parts of the body that have to be covered) is indispensable. He then reminded the audience that, since the time of one's death is not known, postponing wearing the *kerudung* is too risky a speculation. "What would happen to you if you plan to wear it next week, for example, and you die this evening? So, you would be better to wear it as soon as possible," he advised.

Symbolic assertion through clothing also appears among the men of Daarut Tauhid. Although not always, Aa Gym is given to wearing Arabic garments and Pakistani head-coverings. His santri and some of the *jemaah* also most often wear white clothing and the white rimless Arabic cap that is known as *kopeah haji* (hajj cap), for it is commonly worn in Indonesia by those who have done pilgrimage to Mecca. When asked about this particular style of clothing, Aa Gym told me that there was, in fact, no rigid obligation here to wear any particular kind of clothing, "that I wear this [Arabic] clothing is simply to follow my mood. That is, I just put on whichever kind of clothing I wish to." Indeed he often appears in Western-style clothing. So do his *santri* and *jemaah*. This is part of Daarut Tauhid's inclination to abolish the impression that Islamic tradition is incompatible with modernity.

Religious symbols are also obvious in the daily behaviour of men and women at Daarut Tauhid. Islamic phrases for greetings, making promises, complaining, and so forth are commonly applied in daily life. These Islamic, Arabic-sounding phrases, are a prominent part of their ceremonial and daily conversations. Many followers claim that this has a profound impact on the intensity of their religious feeling. An SMA-student follower explained to me his feelings in relation to this.

> My Islamic spirituality increases every time I go shopping at Daarut Tauhid's mini-market. That is intensified by the Islamic atmosphere and phrases used by the shop keepers. When I get inside they approach me by saying *Assalamu'alaikum* (Peace be upon you). Then I feel at peace. When I approach the cashier to pay, he/she addresses me with great hospitality, wishing me luck by saying *Mubarok Mabruk* (May God bless you in things new you have). This makes me feel that shopping here, in contrast to other shopping centres, gives me a sort of religious benefit.

In a wider context, the impact of this tradition of expressing Islamic (Arabic) phrases is similarly felt by the followers. It brings to them an atmosphere that is highly religious, as seen from the following claim of a follower.

> The phrase *Subhanalloh* (The Most Holy Allah) and *Alhamdulillah* (Praise be to Allah), that are most frequently said by people at Daarut Tauhid, makes the atmosphere really Islamic and this effectively intensifies my faith. This is what, in part, drives me to feel like coming back here soon every time I go home. I get religious enjoyment through this sphere of any life.

However, this tendency towards highly religious behaviour is not the whole of life at Daarut Tauhid. One should not be misled into assuming that life there is world-denying. The other part of life at this pesantren is usually viewed as non-religious, and is uncommon in other Islamic centres.

Photograph 10 A pleasant game: followers are devout at the mosque and cheerful on the playing field.

Activities which attract young people are regularly held at Daarut Tauhid. Such activities include sports or games or, under the first-hand leadership of Aa Gym, hiking and camping in mountainous areas. As an ex-*Menwa* member, Aa Gym is said to like *terjun payung* (parachute jumping) and climbing the slopes of mountains (Risnawati 1993:13). That is why he often brings his followers along to mountainous areas. These activities serve as an effective means of channelling into recreation the energies of young people and, at the same time, inculcating

Islamic values. The latter is done, for example, by means of meditative reflection on the mightiness, brilliance, and glory of Allah in creating the universe. Noticeable here is the delicate combination of efforts to satisfy worldly needs and those of meeting religious requirements.

This is also evident in the attention paid at Daarut Tauhid to economic ventures. The thirteen kinds of entrepreneurial activities run from Daarut Tauhid and their rapid development serve as convincing evidence for the attention paid at the pesantren to economic concerns. Muslims at Daarut Tauhid tend to be involved in both religious concerns and business without being preoccupied by either.

Let me end this section by describing an activity practised at Daarut Tauhid at the time I was there, which illustrates the balance of a worldly and an other-worldly orientation.

> The activity is called '*16 Jam Ibadah Bersama Daarut Tauhid*' (16 Hour Ibadah together at Daarut Tauhid). It started at 6 pm on Saturday evening. The 310 participants gathered at that time in the mosque. They performed *shalat Magrib* (Magrib prayer) together. After performing prayers they chanted *wirid* and said *do'a* together. While waiting for the time of *Shalat Isya* (Isya prayer), they recited the Qur'an individually. At about 7.30 pm, they performed *shalat Isya* communally, after which they chanted *wirid* and said *do'a* as after performing *shalat Maghrib*. Then they had dinner together at the mosque with the meal prepared by Daarut Tauhid. Next, after having dinner, they listened to a religious talk delivered by Aa Gym. This ended at 10 pm at which time they went to bed to take a rest, males at a hall and females at the mosque. At 2 am the following morning, the participants came together at the mosque to perform *shalat Tahajjud* (midnight prayer). Then at 3 am they held a reflection led by Aa Gym. The reflection was focused on introspection, reexamining their very existence on the earth. According to Sodikin, this is done "to remember the essence of life and to make sure that they know the reason and the ultimate aim of their existence in the world as Allah's creature, which is nothing but only to perform *ibadah* to Allah." At 4 am, while waiting for the time of *shalat subuh* (dawn prayer), the participants recited the Qur'an privately. When the time came, they performed *shalat subuh* together after which they chanted *wirid* and said *do'a*. Afterwards, they took a rest until 6 am, then had a shower and breakfast. At 6.30 am they started *rihlah* (tour/excursion), walking to a mountainous area. Ending at 10 am, the *rihlah* was comprised of *lintas alam* (cross-country), *Badar* game,[3] consolation games, and other sports. At the *rihlah*, the participants enjoyed recreational tours, games, and sports which are good for both physical and psychological health and

which have an underlying religious orientation. The activities finished at 10 am, completing the 16 hour period.

This example best illustrates the inclination at Daarut Tauhid to reconcile various aspects of life and to see them wholly as the manifestation of *ibadah* (worship/dedication to God). The sixteen hours of activities, which includes sleeping, eating and resting, is considered to be entirely *ibadah*, so it is termed '16 hours *ibadah* together at Daarut Tauhid'. According to Sodikin, the committee chairman,

> sleeping, eating, games, sports, and all other activities in life are necessary parts of life and are intended as a form of *ibadah* sincerely dedicated to Allah. However simple our activity, it can be rewarded as a form of *ibadah*, provided we intend it sincerely as an *ibadah*.

The *ibadah*, which is highly valuable to the eyes of Allah, is therefore not just religious ritual but includes these and the other activities of life when sincerely dedicated to Allah.

Photograph 11 Participants being given instructions and guidance by Aa Gym just before the Badar game starts.

Given this feature of pesantren life at Daarut Tauhid, Dhofier (1980a:xiii) is right in arguing that the pesantren life is, of course, very much concerned with life after death but it is also concerned with life in this world. According to Kyai belief, human fate after death is determined by our conduct and weight of our " *'amal"* (performances of religious rituals and social obligations).

Certainly, this lesson from Daarut Tauhid is another denial against Geertz's (1960:238) view of Islam in the pesantren, criticised by Dhofier,

> as "grave-and-gift" religion (*kuburan dan gandjaran*), for it is primarily concerned with life after death and with the gaining of blessings from God.

Photograph 12 The *rihlah* having just finished, the followers arrive back at the pesantren complex.

4.2 Inner Dynamics: A Harmonious Combination

The balance between the orientation of lives here and in the hereafter leads to an inner sense of harmony felt by Daarut Tauhidians. They profoundly enjoy a harmonious combination between spiritual ecstasy and personal physical happiness.

The heavily spiritually-oriented activities of Islamic rituals practised at Daarut Tauhid generate spiritual ecstasy in the followers. Assuming that they have been fulfilling Allah's commands and avoiding all His prohibitions and that they are thus close to Allah, they feel religiously secure and happy. This assumption of themselves as being sinless has created an inner orderliness since they feel free of the possibility of divine punishment. Furthermore, they have a feeling that Allah is always with them at all times, so that He will always bless and help them. This supplies a number of positive states such as calmness, easiness, stability, courage, optimism, passion and overall personal orderliness.

These positive feelings are particularly important to young Muslims who experience religious crisis as an effect of their modern existence. Juvenile delinquency drives them away from religious piety and social orderliness, which in turn brings about inward uneasiness. In such a state of crisis, they need moral guidance to replace an inner uneasiness with an inner happiness and certainty. This can be found at many religious centres but which commonly ends up by being world-denying. This often traps young people in the dilemma of either being religiously pious, with the consequence of being world-denying, or vice versa, enjoying worldly life with the consequence of ignoring religious guidance.

This conflict between being religious or otherwise in living in the world is bridged at Daarut Tauhid. The non-religious activities there give rise to the inner satisfaction of personal-physical enjoyment deeply felt by these religious young people. They enjoy, for example, personal satisfaction from their involvement in various sports and communal games. This is best exemplified by the *Perang Badar* game, that is part of the '16 Hour *Ibadah*.' While they learn some highly-valued lessons from the *Badar* battle that took place at the time of the Prophet Muhammad, they also enjoy the simulation as a fulfilling game that satisfies their inner demands for such forms of relaxation. While devotion to such games is viewed by nearly all devout Muslims as a waste of time and is generally outside their scope of attention, this kind of activity at Daarut Tauhid has attracted young followers. Through this, they are able to learn that being devout Muslims is dynamic and far from being monotonous in the religiously emotional realm. Thus, being Muslim is by no means divorced from the joy of games and having enjoyed play is by no means necessitates being up-rooted from religious devotion.

While enjoying the consolation games, the young followers also learn some values through play. A final-year primary school student, twelve years of age, commented on this:

> I learned through the game about the battle of *Badar*, in which the Prophet Muhammad was involved, how it would have been, although I just watched without being involved in the game because I am too young. Besides, the game itself is a forum for developing *ukhuwwah Islamiyyah* (Islamic brotherhood).

Creative Expression Eschatological and Worldly Orientations

Photograph 13 An example of game: to put a nail in a bottle

Photograph 14 Another example of a relaxing game

For many followers the game is a form of *riyadhoh*, an Arabic word for exercise, which has the double connotation of physical and psychological exercise. According to a female university student, during the '16 Hour *Ibadah*' she learned the proper way of *ibadah*. According to her, the "proper" *ibadah* "combines Islamic ritual practices and physical exercises as inseparable aspects of life." This *riyadhoh* has brought about an inner dynamic that satisfies the physical and psychological needs of the followers.

4.3 Modesty and Modernity: A Wonderful Combination

The combination is demonstrated more clearly in the way Daarut Tauhid deals with material things. It adopts many aspects of technology without being trapped in the materialistic life. Being modern is often taken to mean living in comfort, while being modest and *sederhana* (simple) seems to mean living in poverty, Daarut Tauhid tries to reconcile these two polarised view points.

Coming into the Daarut Tauhid complex, one might be surprised by the glamour of its mosque, the modern-styled mini-market right beneath the mosque (ground level), and the *wartel* (telephone shop) next to it. The high-standard sound system of the mosque, the computer-equipped official room of the mosque, and a Western-style clock—showing the am-pm time system that is locally uncommon— all of these things in the mosque may surprise visitors. These things might well lead one to consider that Daarut Tauhid is quite modern in outlook.

Photograph 15 The computer centre: for use as well as for rent (taken from *Mangle* December 1993)

This consideration may be further supported by the fact that Daarut Tauhid adopts modern communication equipment. The *kyai*, the *santri pengurus*, and the workers at various businesses are connected by telephones. For local and mobile communication, they also use walky-talkies (hand-held two-way radios) that provide effective and fast connection between them all the time. (This modern communications equipment also allows close relations between males and females at the pesantren, since face-to-face interaction between the two sexes is restricted in Islam because it may lead to adultery.) In addition, Daarut Tauhid has some facsimile machines for internal and external communications.

Close attention to the living areas of both the *kyai* and the *santri* might bring one to the contrasting judgement that life at Daarut Tauhid reflects modesty and simplicity. The *kyai*'s house is not his own but a rented one. He and his family share the house with its owner. Located next to the mosque, it is old in contrast to the mosque. Attached to the house is an "operations room" where *santri* take turns acting as receptionist, welcoming visitors and receiving communications.

The living areas of the *santri* are similarly simple. There is only one new dormitory, where female *santri* are housed, and this is so far the only dormitory that has been built by Daarut Tauhid. The others were formerly houses, are still being rented and have been divided into a series of bedrooms, each of six square metres. Each bedroom is peopled by five to eight santri. The smallness of the rooms is understandable given that Daarut Tauhid is located in an urban area of Bandung. Despite the urban location, both exteriors and interiors of the rooms are very simple. Some are semi-permanent structures while others are permanent. Inside, I found an assortment of beds and mats. This suggests that some inhabitants sleep on beds, while others sleep on the floor. A santri told me that people sleep on beds or the mats on the floor depending on their mood. There are also wardrobes in which the santri store clothes and goods. Additionally, many pieces of clothing are hung on the walls. These and other things in the rooms suggest simplicity.

The rooms are in striking contrast to both the luxurious mosque and to the surrounding houses and buildings. The logic behind this scene is the intention of Aa Gym and his santri to provide evidence of the glory of Allah and their belief in Him and also to demonstrate their nothingness in the face of Allah by their modesty. The luxury of the mosque, as the *baitullah* (house of Allah) is intended to assert the former and the simple rooms, the latter.

However, the simplicity of their rooms, clothing, and overall behaviour does not lead them to the state of Sufistic *zuhud* (asceticism) or to a fatalistic world-denial. In fact, along with their inner dynamics (portrayed above), they also frequently, appear in modern and recent-style clothing, less common among devout Muslims.

Given these two aspects of Daarut Tauhid life, there is no one-sidedness towards either modernity or modesty but a combination of the two. Following a modern style of life does not necessarily mean forgetting religious values and being devoutly religious is not necessarily anti-modern. Daarut Tauhid brings together the values of the two to create an advanced Muslim society and religious modernity.

The application of modern technology is underlined by a cardinal principle held firmly by Daarut Tauhidians, which was summed up by Aa Gym:

> All modern achievement of everything including technology is nothing but Allah's creation. All is but Allah's *nikmat* (courtesy) to human beings. Whoever, Muslim or non-Muslim, discovered scientific advancement is merely Allah's agent in blessing all human beings. Thus, the most worthy human beings to enjoy any of Allah's blessings are none other than *hamba Allah* (Allah's loyal servants), those who believe in and obey Him The Almighty. Muslims have, therefore, first priority and every right to utilise all the advanced achievements of whatever technology. And it is wrong to undermine and deny all of this or otherwise we [Muslims] would remain backward. This is why we try to equip Daarut Tauhid with the most technologically advanced equipment that we can afford.[4]

In anticipating any preoccupation with worldly modernity, Daarut Tauhidians hold to this principle:

> Seek as much knowledge as you can and earn as much wealth as you can but never let them control you. *Ulah kadalon-dalon micinta dunya, sanajan hayoh kaseundeuhan ku dunya, oge hirup tetep basajan* (Never be preoccupied by wealth although you deal with it all the time and be modest in life) (Risnawati 1993:13).

Therefore, while making every attempt to be highly religious, people at Daarut Tauhid also make every effort to achieve a high standard of living in the world. "In short, our mind is one hundred percent *tawekal* (resignation/trust in God) while our body makes the fullest *ikhtiar* (endeavour)," Aa Gym once told me.

4.4 Multi-style Management: A Solid Combination

This combination also extends to the way Daarut Tauhid is managed. Three managerial styles are applied here; military, entrepreneurial, and divine. The combination of these three is readily recognisable through the terms and forms of Daarut Tauhid's activities.

The military style is seen primarily in the terms employed in organisational practices. Every time Aa Gym leaves his home, especially to deliver religious talks, there are always one or two disciples who accompany him. Santri take turns in accompanying Aa Gym. These santri are called *ajudan*, which is an Indonesian military term for guardian or servant.[5] In the military tradition, an *ajudan* serves the *Jenderal* (general). There is thus an impression that, if those accompanying santri are *ajudan*, then Aa Gym is a general. Indeed, along with the santri's awe of Aa Gym's charisma, they appear to respect him as their general. However, this imagery tends to be misleading because Aa Gym himself tends to minimise the hierarchical relationship by treating the *ajudan* as his partners. For instance, he drives his car with the *ajudan* as passengers, something a military general would not do.

Although the term *ajudan* might also reflect the influence of kingly or governmental tradition (see footnote), I believe it is adopted from military tradition both because Aa Gym was a *Menwa* (Student Regiment) commander and because of other military terms used at Daarut Tauhid. The term *komandan* (commander) is also used at Daarut Tauhid in much the same way as it is applied in the Indonesian Armed Forces. The head of the daily picket at the pesantren complex is called *komandan piket*, the head of operational activities is called *komandan lapangan* (field commander), and so forth. The 'operations room' itself reflects the influence of military style, since it is "the model of a military command" which forms part of the "push for integration and unity" in Indonesia (Guinness 1994:272).

Photograph 16 **Participants of the *rihlah* ordered to line up in a military style.**

The military style also appears in the form of activities frequently performed at Daarut Tauhid. The simulation of *perang Badar* is obviously a case in point. Here Aa Gym and his ex-Menwa-member brother, Abdurrahman Yuri, apply their military experiences. The participants practise the military skills of applying strategy and tactics. (Of course, the main aim here is not that of training an army but instead, according to Ikin Sodikin, the chairman of the committee, to teach participants the hardness of the Prophet's struggles in the maintenance of Islam.)

Another activity that gives an impression of military style is highland camping. As a form of recreation, this has its origin, and continues to be practised, in the military tradition. Again, this activity also reflects Aa Gym's former experience in a student regiment.

In addition, the military form of management is also reflected by the dress of the officials of Daarut Tauhid. However, what is adopted at Daarut Tauhid is not the type of the dress but simply the military terms for clothing. They wear three kinds of uniform: PDH (*Pakaian Dinas Harian*, daily uniform), PDU (*Pakaian Dinas Upacara*, ceremonial uniform), and PDL (*Pakaian Dinas Lapangan*, field uniform). These are obviously military terms for dress.

The adoption of a military form of management is said to inculcate the positive value of discipline, which has been successful in the organisation of military life. At Daarut Tauhid it has shown its effectiveness in organising followers as a team and in accelerating the implementation of activities.

The entrepreneurial style is another form of management employed at Daarut Tauhid. It is applied particularly in the economic activities of the pesantren. The pesantren's thirteen business ventures are organised using entrepreneurial techniques. The leader of each unit is called a director.

Although further, detailed investigation of this aspect of Daarut Tauhid's business ventures is needed, I find the economic management of the businesses as applied at Daarut Tauhid to be most modern. The organisation of the mini-market involves up-to-date equipment: the cashier section, for instance, is equipped with modern equipment for storing money and calculating purchases.

In regard to the marketing system, Daarut Tauhid applies modern techniques. It employs some skilful personalities to do this. It also uses cars with which to sell handicrafts and other items produced by its the santri. In addition, advertising is employed to promote its economic and religious activities. Daarut Tauhid uses printed advertisements in addition to the word-of-mouth advertising commonly employed by its followers.

The third managerial style used at Daarut Tauhid is referred to as the *managemen Allah* (divine management). According to Yuri, the military and entrepreneurial styles of management involve divine inspiration and control that guide every action of Daarut Tauhid's organisation. What is meant by "divine management" is that Allah The Almighty is the single "Director," who by His absolute Will develops Daarut Tauhid. Many things have happened at Daarut Tauhid which are not rationally explainable, and which are therefore believed to be proof of the Will of God.

At first glance, the so-called divine management makes Daarut Tauhidians sound fatalistic, as though they totally rely upon Allah's Will and initiate little or even nothing themselves (Karim 1993:63). Yet I think this impression is wrong. Daarut Tauhid's rapid development in every aspect of its activities is enough evidence to counter this impression. One should note that belief in the close involvement of Allah's Will in the development of Daarut Tauhid produces, instead of a fatalistic attitude, a high degree of conviction on the part of the followers that Allah helps and gives his overall blessing to their *ikhtiar* (endeavour). This, in turn, generates in them a profound degree of self-confidence, both in working for Daarut Tauhid in particular and in living in the world in general. Here Allah is mainly viewed as the source of inspiration upon which their works are based. In the meantime, Allah is also viewed as the Supervisor, in that He examines every single action of his followers. Thus, while still working hard, people at Daarut Tauhid are convinced of Allah's guiding inspiration and supervision.

There are two intended aims of divine management. First, Daarut Tauhid aims at developing personally inward discipline to balance military discipline. The latter has the weakness of being highly dependent on other humans, so that an individual might be personally undisciplined in the absence of others' supervision. Dependence on Allah's supervision is effective in countering this possible weakness, and involves the exercise of *kejujuran* (honesty). In every activity, everyone is expected to be honest to himself, to other humans, and to Allah, in the conviction that Allah will always see whatever one hides. An honest Muslim would not cheat although an economic arrangement, for example, may provide a chance for cheating or corruption. Thus, the weakness of human management systems—military and entrepreneurial—can be covered by the divine management.

Second, through divine management Daarut Tauhid also aims at promoting the characteristic of *ikhlash* (sincerity). The main idea of being *ikhlash* is to do everything for the sake of Allah (*Lillahi Ta'ala*). Put another way, whatever a Muslim does has to be sincerely dedicated to Allah. Daarut Tauhidians thus view what they do as their dedication to Allah. This minimises expectations of worldly rewards for what they do.[6] According to Aa Gym, this value of *ikhlash* is "the very key to the rapid growth of Daarut Tauhid."

A conflict arises at Daarut Tauhid concerning the implementation of this value of *ikhlash*. A *santri karyawan* said that Aa Gym tends to rely too much on the quality of *ikhlash* in his employees. Because Aa Gym believes that his employees are truly *ikhlash* (sincere), in that they intend their works as a form of *ibadah* (dedication) to Allah thus expecting less worldly return or wage, he seems to neglect the role of wage and incentives in maintaining the loyalty of the employees. An employee said:

> Too much relying on the *ikhlash*, Aa Gym seems not to consider the competition of employment. He pays his employees below the common standard of wage. He does not worry about the possibility that his employees might resign to look for another employer who pays more. He has to pay at least the same as other employers do. Otherwise, he could lose his employees. I myself may leave my job at Daarut Tauhid to look for a better wage. Besides, I tend to be independent in that I wish to work independently on my own direction.

Apart from such conflict, *ikhlash* has been an integrative part of the divine management that is applied at Daarut Tauhid.

This combination of military, entrepreneurial, and divine styles of management has confirmed the tendency of Daarut Tauhid to combine various orientations in ordering human life. This provides the bases for Daarut Tauhid in actualising its mission as the agent of the reinforcement of Islamic morality in the contemporary world, which will be discussed in the following chapter.

ENDNOTES

[1] Islam does not hold a monopoly on this religious outlook. Brennan R. Hill (1988:63-4) records, for example, that such a dualistic view is common among such religious groups as the Theravada Buddhists and Catholics of the pre- Vatican II period. He also notices that "it still prevails in the more conservative ranks of the church."

[2] One is, I think, justified in getting the impression that these practices sound like Aa Gym's own early religious inclinations, as portrayed in chapter two.

[3] *Badar* game is a simulation in which the participants pretend to be involved in the *Badar* battle at which the Prophet Muhammad was involved.

[4] This confirms the idea that current Islamic resurgences are demonstrated in their basic acceptance and accommodation to modernity (Cantory 1990:183–194).

[5] As a matter of fact, the term *ajudan*, with the same meaning, was also common in the tradition of Indonesian kingdoms and is now perpetuated among high level governmental authorities.

[6] This may confuse one who has read Geertzian concept of *ikhlash* (*iklas*) found among Javanese (Geertz 1960:73). Geertz's definition of *ikhlash* as the "state of willed affectlessness" is obviously misleading. This is because Geertz drew his conception of *ikhlash* from the context of death. Geertz writes that his informant, whose wife had just died, was truly *iklas* in that "he didn't feel anything at all." This, to me, sounds like *sabar* (patience). (For the concept of *sabar*, as understood at Daarut Tauhid, see Chapter Five on the *Qolbun Salim*.)

Chapter 5: Daarut Tauhid as the *Bengkel Akhlaq* Religion and Morality

The phrase *Bengkel Akhlaq* (Workshop for Morality) might remind students of religions that medical practice is often an important feature of Islamic tradition. In Java, in particular, this may be associated with Pesantren Suryalaya in Tasikmalaya, West Java, where Islamic healing is practised (Munawar-Rahman and Ismail 1991, Nurol-Aen 1990, Zulkifli 1994). Horikoshi (1980) has also recorded an Islam-based medical tradition among Sundanese Muslims in Garut town, West Java, that is well-known as *Asrama*.

Suryalaya and *Asrama* practise a rather similar form of Islamic medicine. Suryalaya has, besides wide ranging educational institutions, a centre for the treatment of narcotic addicts and delinquent youths. The patients camp here and thus have no opportunity to think of anything except God (Zulkifli 1994:111). Su'dan (1991:75-77) describes that in the camp the patients perform *mandi taubat* (baths for repentance), obligatory *shalat* five times a day, a series of recommended *shalat* such as *sunnat tahajjud, sunnat tasbih*, and *sunnat witir* at night, *sunnat dhuha* in the morning and *sunnat rawatib* performed before and after obligatory *shalat*. They also have to perform Sufistic *dhikir* (remembrance of God), both *dhikir jahar* (loud *dhikir*) and *dhikir khafi* (*dhikir* in a very low tone). Given these practices, Suryalaya appears to be a clinic that involves the restoration of both physiological and religious order in the patient.

Daarut Tauhid shares one feature with this Islamic tradition, that is, the restoration of Islamic values in its followers as a means by which to create righteous Muslims. However, compared to Suryalaya, Daarut Tauhid's function as the workshop for morality is unique for several reasons. First, Daarut Tauhid does not practise physical healing such as the *mandi taubat* practised at Suryalaya. It practises, instead, psycho-religious healing in that it provides religious activities where Muslims suffering from immorality can indirectly "modify" their daily behaviour. Second, the "patients" at Daarut Tauhid are, as a result, more active than those at Islamic healing centres such as Suryalaya. They do not come to Daarut Tauhid to be cured as patients but to participate in religious practices that have the impact of psychological curing. The process of curing is thus, in a sense, an indirect one. Third, the object of the healing at Daarut Tauhid is the social and behavioural ills, some of which cannot be easily felt as an illness unless they are viewed from the Islamic point of view.[1] Here, Daarut Tauhid's conception of moral decadence is crucial and thus deserves particular attention.

5.1 Moral Decadence

Before describing how Daarut Tauhid runs its mission as the *Bengkel Akhlaq*, it is important to understand what Daarut Tauhidians perceive as moral decadence. There are two reasons for this. First, what is viewed by Daarut Tauhidians as morally decadent might not be so in the view of others. Second, it would be difficult to follow a process of healing without knowing the problem that it attempts to rectify.

Moral decadence, to people at Daarut Tauhid, is none other than the decline of religiosity and the social disorder it engenders. People of the world today tend to be less religious and are heavily preoccupied by worldly business. They show little or no awe and indebtedness to God, who provides all worldly delights and who created all beings other than Himself. According to Aa Gym, this tendency of men and women today is due to the fact that they are preoccupied by their carnal desires. This can be seen through their daily behaviour.

First, people today appear to have a lust for prestige, praise, appreciation, pomp, honour, self-esteem and the like. In gaining these, they tend to follow the evil instructions which cunningly use these personal interests as a weapon to drive human beings away from the right path of Islam. For the sake of honour and self-esteem, for example, people try to impress others by wearing the most expensive suits and driving the most luxurious cars. They never hesitate to spend any amount of money just to realise their aim of being appreciated and esteemed, without thinking of any risk to their *hisab* (accountability)[2] in the hereafter.

Aa Gym clarified that this by no means signifies that people are not allowed to look nice because, he argued, looking good is good and Allah loves everything good. Syeikh Abdul Qadir Jailani, a great Sufi and a traditional *ulama*, tended to look clean and impressive. But, at the same time, he was fully aware of his *hisab* in the hereafter. He thus differed from people nowadays who ignore this *hisab*. These latter, while giving only a little *shidqah* (charity) or perhaps none at all for the sake of the poor, spend a lot of money shopping for themselves in the highest quality supermarkets. They seem to be heartless. They come only rarely, if ever, to religious centres whereas they routinely go on distant and thus expensive trips. They, in short, tend to pay nearly all their attention to worldly and short-term enjoyment, ignoring moral and religious values.

The lust for self-esteem and prestige often also makes one over-react. When angry, for example, a person tends to over-react, showing others that he is in charge and in power. He might also trivialise and underestimate others just to assert his own reputation. This is, Aa Gym pointed out, just a means by which "Satan brings misfortune to human beings, in that human beings become *takabbur* (haughty). The key to overcoming this is *tawadhu'* (modesty) since honour generates not from *takabbur* but from *tawadhu'*." Aa Gym also asserted that "as a matter of fact, people are resentful of one who is haughty, arrogant, and self-assertive by way of mentioning his superiority."

Second, Daarut Tauhidians find that people of today tend also to give their passion free rein and enjoy their life to the fullest without thanking God, who provides the grace for all beings. People let their bodily senses relish all worldly things beyond the normal standard and without having any care for other beings. Indeed, Aa Gym realises that human bodily senses love to enjoy various things to the fullest. The sense of enjoying food, for instance, drives Muslims today to eat as many delicious things as possible, without any consideration of whether these things are *halal* or *haram* in accordance with Islamic teaching. In addition to this enjoyment of food, people also tend to use their mouths to talk too much. While talking too much, they often tell lies, gossip about others, sully the names of others, and talk about other matters that often engender inharmonious social relationships.

Similarly, in the view of Aa Gym, to satisfy the enjoyment of their ears people tend to love listening to music more than listening to *pengajian* or the melodious recitation of Holy Qur'an. Men's eyes greatly enjoy watching beautiful sights and pleasant views, without remembering Allah as the Creator of the universe that amazes them. The men's eyes particularly enjoy watching beautiful women, just for sexual satisfaction and thus often resulting in sexual abuse. Sexuality is also often the main interest of a young couple in love, with no thought of realising pure love in accordance with the religious guidance about love. In short, people nowadays, according to Aa Gym, tend to live a life that the Qur'an calls *mata' al-gurur* (goods and chattels of deception) (3:185).[3]

According to Aa Gym, enjoyment should be in moderation without any inclination towards excess. "Following one's passion in such enjoyment," Aa Gym said, "is like drinking sea water; the more one drinks the more thirsty one will be." To stop talking too much, according to Aa Gym's advice, one has to do *tadarrus* (recite, usually loudly) the holy Qur'an more often. To stop over eating, one is recommended by Islam to fast. Other Islamic teachings deal similarly with social disorders.

But, unfortunately, this social impact of Islam has been obscured by the third phenomenon of Muslims today. This, according to people at Daarut Tauhid, is that Muslims tend to be reluctant to carry out Islamic teachings. For example, they seem to find it difficult to perform *shalat*, particularly midnight *shalat*. They also feel it is difficult to go to the mosque, either to perform *shalat* or to attend public talks or any other gatherings. They also consider it hard to read the holy Qur'an, so that they are far away from its guidance. They find it difficult to give *shidqah* or, if they do, they often do it with the underlying motivation of *riya* (doing things just for fashion) in the hope of human valuation. For Daarut

Tauhidians, all this reluctance in applying Islamic teachings has been the chief factor that has caused current social ills to proliferate.

Further, they see that juvenile delinquency and overall social immorality today are primarily caused by the individual disorders of men and women. Their hearts and minds have been contaminated by the lust to gain the fullest enjoyment from living, which is often socially or personally detrimental. In this situation, *iri-dengki* (envy and hatred) is a commonly suffered ill. Aa Gym defined *iri-dengki* as a state when "one feels uncomfortable to see others achieve good luck and, conversely, one feels great happiness when they lose it or even suffer from bad luck." Aa Gym maintains that envy is a psychological ill that often drives one to detrimental actions. He further identifies envy as "the basic character of *iblis* (devil, Satan). *Iblis* refused to perform *sujud* (prostration to pay homage) to Adam, when Allah asked him to, because *iblis* was very envious of the status given to Adam by Allah. One who easily becomes envious and spiteful has therefore adopted this basic character of *iblis*."

In the view of Aa Gym, there are four main causes that can engender envy. The first is enmity or hatred. In this situation, one may easily feel disadvantaged by an opponent. Envy often easily arises here. Second is the personal interest in being the best. Aa Gym gave an example that "a person who has been wearing his most expensive clothes may be envious just because he sees a man wearing better-looking clothes. He may then feel defeated and hate the man just because of jealousy." Third is personal ambition for leadership. This often drives one to hate others who have a good career as leader. "If he hears of a leader with a high reputation and who is greatly admired, he will be more and more envious, wishing to put him down," Aa Gym explained. That is why, according to Aa Gym, the first group to enter hell will be "those envious *ulama* who are always ambitious to be leaders and always seeking popularity." Fourth is that envy can be caused by other *akhlaq buruk* (bad character traits). One who is stingy, for example, might be jealous of someone who gains good luck as a result of his generosity.

Just like *iri-dengki*, there are many other social ills that are viewed by Daarut Tauhidians to be mushrooming among men and women today. Inferiority, anxiety, and overall uneasiness are now common feelings suffered by marginalised people. Arrogance, haughtiness, *riya* and *sum'ah* [4] are common characteristics among the people of high social status. Both groups tend to abandon their religious ethics, ignoring the role of Allah in their lives. As a result, each group has been trapped into bad habits such as prejudice, stereotyping, *ghibah* (gossip), and searching for each other's humiliation. In short, people today are, in the view of Aa Gym and his followers, in severe moral crisis.

Aa Gym has been successful in convincing Muslims of this moral crisis. He convinces them through various religious talks at Daarut Tauhid and other Islamic gatherings, on radio programs, and through his writings in Daarut Tauhid's weekly newsletter. These become his forum by which he can effectively use his rhetorical ability to disseminate his views on moral decadence and its Islamic resolution.

Aa Gym believes that the key to this resolution is ordering the individual mind and heart. The grand target of Daarut Tauhid is thus to restore Islamic morality in the hearts and minds of people today.

5.2 *Qolbun Salim*: Qualities of Heart and Mind

Qolbun is an Arabic word for heart or mind, while *salim* is an Arabic term denoting healthy, sound, or good. *Qolbun salim* thus literally means healthy heart or sound mind.[5] Daarut Tauhid's use of the phrase *qolbun salim* is said to be derived from verses of the Qur'an which read:

Yauma laa yanfa'u maalun	The Day whereon neither wealth
walaa banuun	nor sons will avail,
illaa man atallaaha	but only he [will prosper] that brings to Allah
bi qolbin saliim	a sound heart.
(26:88–89)	
Idz Jaa-a robbahuu	Behold, he [Abraham] approached his Lord
bi qolbin saliim	with a sound heart.
(37:84)	

The phrase *qolbun salim* is mentioned in the Qur'an twice in the two verses quoted above. By *qolbun salim* Aa Gym means a heart that is pure and unaffected by the moral ills that afflict others. It is a personal condition which is free from bad characteristics that are both personally and socially dangerous. Being pure, the *qolbun salim* is full of good characteristics and motivation in this world.

Daarut Tauhidians have been striving to achieve the quality of *qolbun salim* in two ways. The first is freeing their minds from any bad thoughts and characteristics and the other is adopting as high a degree of good character as they can. In terms of the former, Daarut Tauhidians free themselves from bad characteristics such as arrogance, inferiority, prejudice, *riya* (doing things just for fashion), *iri-dengki* (envy), and so on, which are all viewed as decadent.

Being free from such bad character traits, Muslims at Daarut Tauhid make every attempt to adopt high standards of personal qualities which are necessary to achieve a perfect heart, *qolbun salim*. The very basis for *qolbun salim* is a strong grasp of *tauhid* (the oneness of Allah). As there is only one God in which to believe, Daarut Tauhidians totally rely on Him. A follower, echoing Aa Gym, said:

> Allah is the absolute ruler of the universe. He is the only one who determines every single occurrence. Therefore, we rely totally on His power and make every effort to seek His guidance and help. Unless Allah guides and helps us, who else might be able to do so since He is the absolute power that rules our life.

Indeed, *tauhid* is the main aspect of Islam which is always asserted by Aa Gym on every occasion. Each time he starts his talk, for example, he always spends some time reminding his audience of this *tauhid*. The following prologue of a *pengajian* is an example:

> Praise be to Allah, The only Being that blesses all other beings. Allah can not be seen by human eyes but can be easily recognised by *mata hati* (the mind's eye) which is full of the pure *iman* (faith). Allah is the most perfect essence. His knowledge covers all other kinds of knowledge. By His omniscience, he creates this wonderful universe with all things in it including humans. Humans and other beings are very weak without the power given by Allah the Absolute Power. He is very close to us, watching our every movement. And, surely, He is witnessing our gathering here now as a form of our devotion to Him.

Consequently, *tauhid* is always the main message of every Aa Gym talk at public *pengajian*, on radio, and elsewhere.[6] Aa Gym insists that the oneness of God and the consequent reliance on Him alone has to be the basic conviction that is deeply inculcated in the mind and heart of every Muslim. Without this, it is said, the human mind and heart would remain full of bad thoughts that result in bad behaviour.

Based on this total conviction of the oneness of God, Muslims at Daarut Tauhid attribute all their good traits to the inspiration of Islam. Several main character traits are highly "promoted" at Daarut Tauhid. *Ikhlash* (sincerity) is the *first* quality that is often brought to the fore. Men and women at Daarut Tauhid believe that *ikhlash* has to colour their minds and hearts to gain the level of *qolbul salim*. The proper belief in *tauhid* must generate one's *ikhlash* in living in the world. *Ikhlash*, a follower explained, is actually "absolute reliance on and acting only for the sake of Allah." A Muslim's mind has thus to be independent from anything and anyone other than Allah. Muslims do something sincerely for the sake of Allah and similarly they refrain from doing certain things for the sake of Allah.

Aa Gym said that those *Mukhlishin* (sincere people) are the only group that Satan can not deceive. He referred to a verse of Qur'an in this regard:

> Satan said: O my Lord! because You have put me in the wrong, I will make (wrong) fair-seeming to them on the earth and I will put them all in the wrong except the sincere servants among them (15:39–40)

Therefore, to Aa Gym, the most effective way to ward off Satan's attempts to deceive is to do everything with the underlying tone of *ikhlash*, sincerely dedicated for the sake of Allah. He further elaborated:

> Never do anything in the hope of others' admiration and appreciation because human admiration and appreciation are nothing compared to those which come from God. There is no point in expecting human acclamation since we know that human beings can praise only if Allah facilitates them to do so. If Allah does not allow one to praise us, we would lose a lot because while no one acclaims us Allah gives us nothing. What a pity! So, stop expecting human admiration. Do everything sincerely for the sake of Allah.[7]

The *second* quality that is believed by Daarut Tauhidians to construct *qolbun salim* is *tawadhu'* (modesty). If *takabbur* (to be haughty) is seen by Aa Gym as a source of degradation, *tawadhu'* is, on the contrary, a source of honour. "Honour is not generated from *takabbur* but from *tawadhu'*," he said. In this regard a follower said that to be modest is actually a hard job because humans naturally love to be praised and, unfortunately, they find being physically impressive is the best way to gain this praise. People forget, according to this follower, that demonstrating good manners, including being modest, is the most effective way to be honoured. Even so, he continued, a modest person is respectable not merely before humans but also, and this is the most important, before Allah. "What is the point of being honoured by humans but degraded by Allah?" he asked.

In a conversation on modesty, a *santri* said that Aa Gym often told the *santri* and the *jemaah* of Daarut Tauhid that forgiving one who had done one some wrong is a form of modesty which is highly recommended in Islam. In the Qur'an, he said, Allah insists many times that he promises to esteem greatly anyone who willingly forgives others' wrongdoings towards him. The *santri* then quoted a Hadith said to have been once told by Aa Gym:

> The Prophet Muhammad said: "Wealth never decreases because of *shidqah* (charity). Allah will always bless with high esteem anyone who forgives others. As well, Allah guarantees that one who is modest for the sake of Allah will be a person worthy of deep esteem.

Indeed, Aa Gym himself said that "people are nauseated by haughty persons and they, instead, hold modest persons in high esteem."

The *third* personal quality that is often brought to the fore is *jujur* (honesty). A *qolbun salim* is a heart that is free from any lie and is, instead, full of honesty. Honesty is viewed by Daarut Tauhidians as the very key to good social and personal relationships. This is because humans, unlike God, cannot recognise the true intentions of others. Unless one is honest enough, one could tell a lie to others. One's honesty is thus extremely important to the establishment of good human relationships. A business affair, for instance, will never run well without each party's high quality of personal honesty. Indeed, honesty is universally a basic element of an individual's trustworthiness.

Fourth, *sabar* (patience) is also seen as an important character of *qolbun salim*. According to Aa Gym, *sabar*, together with *shalat*, is the way by which Allah guides Muslims. Here he referred to verses of the Holy Qur'an in which Allah says:

> O you who believe, seek help with patient perseverance and prayer for Allah is with those who patiently persevere (2:153).

> Be sure we shall test you with something of fear and hunger, some loss in goods, lives, and the fruits (of your toil), but give glad tidings to those who patiently persevere; who say, when afflicted with calamity, "To Allah we belong and to Him is our return" (2:155–156).

Patience is extremely important in facing the problems of life, and being patient in facing problems is highly rewarded by Allah. Therefore, in the view of Aa Gym, "patience is a form of *amal shaleh* (good deeds) that is very relevant to receiving Allah's guidance." Using analogy, Aa Gym said that a patient Muslim is like diamond in its resistance. He explained that when a diamond is hit by a stone, for example, it will resist and may even look more sparkling instead of being broken. Meanwhile, the stone which hit it might be smashed to pieces. Thus, a patient man will be resistant to any test and temptation of life.

Aa Gym further asserted the important role *sabar* should play in two situations. First, patience is undeniably crucial in facing life's problems. In this case, according to Aa Gym,

> one has to learn patiently every *hikmah* (lesson) behind the problems faced. First, life's problems might be a warning from Allah either against one's immorality and sin or against one's greed in expecting more gifts of grace while never thanking Allah for what has already been given by Allah. Second, the problems might be a means by which Allah shields one from things that may bring misfortune. Finally, it might also be a chance for one to enjoy the help and patronage of Allah.

Sabar thus here seems to be both following reason and restraining oneself from sadness, desire, fear, anger and other emotional burdens.

Second, perfect patience is extremely helpful in *ikhtiar* (working hard). In making an effort, Aa Gym said, one should not depend on anyone other than Allah. If one employs anything or asks help from others, one has to intend it as a fulfilment of Allah's teaching to work hard, so that Allah is the only One to depend on. One's total reliance on Allah should make one confident and perseverant because of one's high conviction of Allah's presence and aid. Thus *sabar* does not at all mean passivity, as Geertz found among Javanese *priyayi* (1960:241), but active striving to do one's best in the way of Allah.

These are the main character traits that men and women at Daarut Tauhid have been trying to adopt as part of their effort to make their hearts sound and perfect (*qolbun salim*). There are of course other noble characteristics that they constantly attempt to adopt, and that are included in Aa Gym's message in every talk. Aa Gym also insists that the adoption of these good character traits has to be intended as a form of one's obedience to Allah's command. Without this intention of obedience, being a good person will not be rewarded as a good deed. Thus, according to a santri, *akhlaq* (morality) has always to be related to *iman* (faith) as suggested by the following Hadith:

> The most perfect of the faithful in faith is the most beautiful of them in character. I was sent [as a prophet] to complete the beautiful character traits.

A *qolbun salim* has to possess perfect faith which turns out to be the most beautiful character traits in one's behaviour. Aa Gym's chief orientation to ordering the heart and mind is made clearer through the tradition of *pengajian*, which is known as the *Taushiyah Penyejuk Hati*.

5.3 *Taushiyah Penyejuk Hati*

The tradition of *pengajian* is as common in Sundanese West Java as in other parts of Indonesia. Horikoshi (1976) noted that *pengajian* is part of the Islamic tradition in Garut. In Bandung this tradition is no less common. Though the term *pengajian* originally refers to any learning activity, religious or secular, it is now becoming more specific and refers to learning religious instructions in a social gathering (Horikoshi 1976:133) held at a mosque, *pesantren*, house, or any public building. Here tens, hundreds, or even thousands of Muslims listen to a religious talk delivered by a *kyai* or a *muballigh* (preacher).

At Daarut Tauhid such *pengajian* is known as *Taushiyah Penyejuk Hati* (Comforting Religious Advice). This term was deliberately chosen to reflect the primary target of Daarut Tauhid, that is the achievement of *qolbun salim*. By this *Taushiyah Penyejuk Hati* Daarut Tauhid aims to help those Muslims in attendance to achieve the quality of *qolbun salim*.

The *Taushiyah Penyejuk Hati* is held at Daarut Tauhid on a twice-weekly basis; on Sunday afternoons at 1.30 PM and on Thursday evenings at 7 PM. In addition, Aa Gym regularly gives *Taushiyah Penyejuk Hati* on two radio channels in Bandung. That is on 106.5 Antassalam FM on Mondays at 6.30 PM and on Medinatussalam FM on Thursdays at 9.30 PM.

The *Taushiyah Penyejuk Hati* that is held at Daarut Tauhid is, of course, distinguished by two features. First, it was the origin of the emergence of Daarut Tauhid itself. As noted earlier in Chapter Two, Pesantren Daarut Tauhid developed from a small group of *pengajian*. Second, the attendance of a large number of followers, which reflects this program's attractiveness, suggests that the *Taushiyah Penyejuk Hati* is more important than any other single activity. The followers find listening directly to the *Taushiyah Penyejuk Hati* at Daarut Tauhid more satisfactory than listening to it on the radio. Some followers told me that they came to Daarut Tauhid to attend the *Taushiyah Penyejuk Hati* after they had listened to it on the radio. A follower said that "Aa Gym's religious talk on the radio was very impressive, but listening to it directly here at Daarut Tauhid is to me more impressive." When asked why, he answered "I do not know." But he then explained that it may be because of the direct contact with Aa Gym and the large number of Muslims in attendance. He felt, he said, a spiritual satisfaction from seeing Aa Gym as a religious example of life. He also obtained a feeling of religious solidarity from getting together with other Muslims in such large numbers. Thus, to this follower and to others, gathering together on the occasion of *Taushiyah Penyejuk Hati* at Daarut Tauhid makes closer their relation to Aa Gym and to other Muslim brothers and sisters.[8]

Moreover, the *Taushiyah Penyejuk Hati* is more important than the Friday service given by Daarut Tauhid. There is no doubt that the Friday service is usually the most important event in the Muslim world. This is well-illustrated, for example, by Bowen (1993:296) who shows how "the Friday service in the Takengen [Aceh] mosque structures the week's activities for men and women living in nearby villages." However, the Friday service is less important at Daarut Tauhid. This is, I observed, for the main reason that Aa Gym is rarely present at Friday service time. He is usually invited to deliver Friday sermon at other mosques. (Daarut Tauhid itself usually invites other Muslims of learning to deliver the Friday sermon there.)

The presence of Aa Gym is profoundly important to the followers' attendance. It significantly determines the size of the audience. This was brought to my attention when Aa Gym was performing the *umrah* (the lesser pilgrimage) to Mecca from December the 19th 1994 to January the 4th 1995. In the absence of Aa Gym, the number of the followers attending the *Taushiyah Penyejuk Hati* decreased by more than half. The mosque was less than half filled. Many followers did not come although Daarut Tauhid had by then invited some prominent *muballigh* (preachers) to replace Aa Gym during his absence. This certainly demonstrates the degree to which Aa Gym is important to his followers.[9] This is why the *Taushiyah Penyejuk Hati*, which is delivered by Aa Gym personally, is more important an event than the Friday service at Daarut Tauhid, the sermon of which is not delivered by Aa Gym.

Although the *Taushiyah Penyejuk Hati* on Sundays formally begins at 1.30 PM, some of the audience come as early as 12 PM, which is the due time for performing *shalat dhuhur* (afternoon worship). Those who come this early usually perform *shalat dhuhur* together with the santri. Aa Gym acts as the *imam* of the *shalat* if he is available. The most frequent case finds Aa Gym most often fulfilling some invitation to preach outside Daarut Tauhid. Those who come later have commonly performed *shalat dhuhur* at home or at a neighbouring mosque. When entering the Daarut Tauhid's mosque, they commonly perform the optional *shalat* of two cycles, which is recommended by Islam to respect the mosque as a holy place and is thus called *shalat tahiyyatul masjid* (greeting the mosque).

Photograph 17 A few followers, who have come early for the *Taushiyah Penyejuk Hati*, recite the Qur'an or perform the optional *shalat*.

The audience arrives individually, in pairs, or in a group. They gradually fill the three storey mosque, men on the first floor and women on the second.[10] As the second floor is narrower than the first and since women slightly outnumber the men, some women fill roughly a quarter of the first floor, on the right behind a piece of green fabric draped between the mosque's pillars. (This fabric is set as high as a sitting person during the *Taushiyah Penyejuk Hati* and as a standing person during *shalat*.) The audience seem to come as early as they can to claim the closest possible position to the mimbar from which Aa Gym will deliver the *Taushiyah Penyejuk Hati*.

By about 1 PM, the mosque has usually been filled by the audience. Those who come after this time usually have to use the back part of the mosque, its stairs, or the yard and the street in front of the mosque. The santri appear busy ordering the audience in the mosque; asking them to fill any gaps to give room for those coming later. Outside the mosque, some santri roll out mats on which those who cannot come into the mosque can sit. Two santri are busy ordering traffic, since the narrow street in front of the mosque is crowded by the followers, other pedestrians, passing cars, pedicabs, and motorcycles. Other santri are busy managing the parking of the cars and motorcycles of the followers, since many of them come by their own transportation.

While waiting for the commencement of the *Taushiyah Penyejuk Hati* at 1.30 PM, the audience are recommended to do *tadarrus* (reciting Qur'an) individually. It is interesting the way this recommendation is done. Rather than an announcement through the loud speaker system, the organising santri simply distribute a huge number of the holy Qur'an, which are available at every corner of the mosque to the audience by passing them along from a person to another until each one gets a copy. This has been the tradition and without any explanation, each starts doing *tadarrus* of their own.

Photograph 18 Many followers come by motorbike or car.

About ten minutes before 1.30 PM, an organising santri asks the followers to stop *tadarrus*. The Qur'an are then passed back along to the corners of the mosque. This santri then calls on the followers to chant *al-Asma al-Husna*.[11]

This *al-Asma al-Husna* is sung together with an impressive melody. The santri leads the chanting. They sing the long *al-Asma al-Husna* without any text. Therefore, the leading santri must sing it by heart. Some followers seem to sing it by heart, while others seem simply to follow. The massive chanting produces a thunderous yet melodious sound. (One would enjoy it as I did.)

The chanting of *al-Asma al-Husna* is not intended to be a mere song to fill the time of waiting. It is, a santri said, intended to intensify the faith of the followers in the *tauhid*. By chanting the *al-Asma al-Husna* the followers can remember Allah with these ninety-nine attributes of His superiority.

The chanting of the *al-Asma al-Husna*, stops precisely at 1.30 PM. Then a santri comes up to host the formal program. He begins by greeting the audience saying *as-salamu 'alaikum wa rahmatullahi wa barakatuh* (peace be to you and the mercy and blessing of Allah). Next he thanks Allah, praising Him and asserting His oneness and His absolute power, and he asks Allah to bless the Prophet Muhammad. Afterwards, he makes some announcements concerning the current activities of Daarut Tauhid. When finished, he invites a santri to chant some verses of the Qur'an. These verses are then translated into Indonesian by another santri.[12] After this brief opening ceremony, Aa Gym comes into the mosque and mounts the mimbar to give religious advice. (If Aa Gym comes late to the mosque, because he has been delivering a religious talk elsewhere, the waiting time would be spent singing *al-Asma al-Husna* together or reciting *tadarrus* individually.)

The following is an example of Aa Gym's speech on Sunday 11 December 1994. After opening remarks thanking and praising Allah for His continuous blessing upon humans and saying *sholawat* for the Prophet Muhammad, Aa Gym began his talk by saying

> Men and women who do not know Allah well would depend heavily on humans or things other than Allah. They fear the creatures instead of fearing the Creator. They also hope for blessing from them not from Allah. As a result, many of those people live in misery. Do they not realise that everything depends on Allah? Though some one is willing to give you something, for example, he/she will not give you anything unless Allah allows him/her to do so. That is because verily it is Allah who determines our life. Note that all creatures *la haula wa la quwwata illa billahil 'aliyyil 'adziem* [have neither power nor energy unless they are given them by Allah, the High, the Inaccessible].

This prologue, again, demonstrates Aa Gym's insistence on the complete belief in *tauhid* and in the consequent superiority of Allah.

Aa Gym then went on to advise the audience of how much Allah loves His beloved Muslims. First of all, he reminded the audience of the fact that only a few Muslims are aware of the truth that ultimate happiness is being beloved by Allah.

> Of course one must be happy when given wealth, position, title, award, and the like. But, you know, these things are given by Allah to everyone, Muslim or not, pious or not. Therefore, one's achievement of those things does not indicate Allah's favour and love. We do not want, of course, to achieve this worldly enjoyment without Allah's favour and love. This is because we learn what Allah says in the Qur'an: *Inna akromakum 'indallahi atqokum* [Verily, the most honoured of you in the sight of Allah is he who is the most righteous of you].[13]

Aa Gym then mentioned some indications by which one can recognise Allah's favour. One of these indications is worth noting here.

> Dear *sahabat* (friends), an indication of Allah's favour and love is the cleanliness of one's mind and heart. Allah will always make the mind and heart of His beloved Muslims free from any bad character and interests. When one's mind is very pure (*bening*), Allah will make it easy for one to grasp high knowledge that cannot be grasped by other people. In grasping knowledge, a Muslim with clean mind is like one who digs land to build a well. While digging, a spring (*mata air*) suddenly spouts out from the depth of the land. There would be a sudden flow of high knowledge that is blessed by Allah as a reward to the Muslim for having a clean mind. This sound mind is like a completely clean mirror without any spots on it. People will love to make this person a mirror that they can use as an example for living. On the contrary, one with a dirty mind is just like a dirty mirror; none would refer to him. Further, the clean mind is reflected through good manners, good language, good ways of looking, and other behaviour. It is also reflected through the outcome of ideas. Excellent ideas will only come from a sound mind while only crazy ideas would come from a dirty mind. It is like a teapot or bottle. If it is filled with tea, it will produce tea, if coffee coffee, if alcohol alcohol, and so forth. Thus, whether one is good or bad, the way one behaves depends on whether one's mind is good or bad.

Aa Gym's advice continues on in this vein throughout the *Taushiyah Penyejuk Hati*. This usually ends by the time of *shalat ashar* (afternoon worship).

It is interesting that Aa Gym, in the middle of his talk, often has very short breaks of about 30 seconds to a minute, during which he commands the audience to either do *istighfar* or recite *sholawat*. This kind of break is particularly frequent during question time, as Aa Gym needs some time to read the audience's questions before responding. During each break the members of the audience individually say *istighfar* or *sholawat* just as Aa Gym has commanded. These short breaks, with what is done therein, are very significant in bringing the audience to a state of sadness, a situation that is "built" by Aa Gym for the following ritual.

5.4 Ritual Weeping: Nature and Structure

The most distinct feature of Pesantren Daarut Tauhid, not found at other Islamic centres, is the tradition of ritual weeping. This is a tradition in the sense that it is established as a custom. The *kyai* Aa Gym and his followers frequently cry during both individual and communal rituals.

People at Daarut Tauhid frequently cry during rituals but they are not possessed. Usually they cry in a sitting position, most often by covering their faces with both hands. They simply cry, their eyes glistening with tears or teardrops. They cry in a normal way and only rarely wail. I only once saw a follower wail copiously in a Sunday ritual, as if facing a beloved person's death. This follower embraced Aa Gym emotionally, thanking Aa Gym for making him religiously conscious and begging Aa Gym to ask Allah's forgiveness for all his sins in his life in the past. (This follower seemed to be a newcomer and this was perhaps why he cried excessively, being emotionally touched by the ritual for the first time.) After some time embracing Aa Gym, he sat back and remained crying with his head bent down. Note that in his weeping there was no sign of this follower being possessed.

The tradition of ritual weeping at Daarut Tauhid can be differentiated into communal and individual forms. The communal can be further divided into that which is regular and that which is irregular. The communal, regular tradition of ritual weeping is held twice weekly; following the *Taushiyah Penyejuk Hati* on Sundays and Thursdays. On these occasions, gatherings of no less than two thousand followers cry profusely. The communal, irregular tradition of ritual weeping takes place occasionally at Daarut Tauhid's workshops. This tradition is best exemplified by the program of *16 jam Ibadah bersama di Daarut Tauhid*, described in Chapter Four.

The individual tradition of ritual weeping takes place particularly during meditative reflection. Men and women at Daarut Tauhid are used to reflecting late in the night following midnight *shalat*. This individual tradition of ritual weeping also takes place after every *shalat*, both obligatory and optional. It is really hard to find anyone who has performed *shalat* at Daarut Tauhid without crying afterwards.

The tradition of ritual weeping, which is communal and regularly observed on Sundays at Daarut Tauhid, is brought to the fore here to provide an illustration. The ritual begins with the performance of *Shalat Ashar* communally. Just before the *shalat* is commenced, Aa Gym, as the *imam*, says some words to remind the followers of how the *shalat* should be personally affective and thus effective. This is certainly a distinctive occurrence. It is true that, in modern Muslim tradition, it is customary for the *imam* to say a few words. However, rather than reminding the followers of the supposed impact of the *shalat* performance, the *imam* simply commands the followers to perform the *shalat* in the correct order, such as straightening the line of followers. Thus, while other *imam* focus only on the exoteric form of the *shalat*, that is physical performance, Aa Gym leads his followers to the esoteric effect. This is part of Aa Gym's attempt to prepare the followers to exercise their feelings.

Then, during the *shalat* performance, Aa Gym tries to bring the followers into a state of sadness. This is done by the way he recites the Qur'anic verses and the prayers in the *shalat*. He recites them with an underlying tone of sadness. In *Shalat Ashar* (Afternoon Worship), as in other *shalat* that are performed during the daytime, these verses and prayers are recited in a soft and deep voice. Nevertheless, with the help of a good sound system, the followers can still hear Aa Gym's sad voice in the *shalat* recitations. Aa Gym's sad voice is heard more effectively in night *shalat*, such as *Shalat Isya* (After Sunset Worship) which is part of the Thursday ritual, because in these night *shalat* these verses and prayers are recited loudly.

This style of Aa Gym's performance of *shalat* makes the followers fall into this pensive and sad feeling. Many followers cry during their *shalat* performance. I could hear the sad tone of the followers next to me during the *shalat*. Tears can also be found on the faces of the followers after the performance of *shalat*. The performance of *shalat* with weeping is certainly an extremely rare experience. It is believed that highly devout Muslims may perform *shalat* with tears. Yet, in my experience, I have never seen a Muslim crying in *shalat* except at Daarut Tauhid. Moreover, the *shalat* with tears at Daarut Tauhid is not merely an individual phenomenon but a communal one.

When the *shalat* is completed, Aa Gym leads the followers to chant *wirid*. The *wirid* chanted here is, in fact, as simple as that commonly chanted by other Muslims. However, Aa Gym makes some modifications that assert his inclination to the *tauhid*. The following is an example of a *wirid* led by Aa Gym. First, Aa Gym, echoed by the followers, chanted *Surah al-Fatihah*, the first chapter of the Qur'an, once. Then he chanted

Allohu la ilaaha illaa anta	O Allah, there is no god but You
La ilaaha illaa hua	There is no god but Him
al-hayyu al-qoyyuum	the Living the Self-Subsisting

This part of the *wirid* is a modification of Aa Gym's and is less commonly practised after *shalat*. It clearly suggests the *tauhid*. He further chanted the last three chapters of the Qur'an; *Al-Ikhlas* (the Purity of Faith, Chapter 112), *Al-Falaq* (the Dawn, Chapter 113), and *An-Nas* (Mankind, Chapter 114). It should be noted that these three chapters of the Qur'an are verses of *tauhid*. These chapters of the Qur'an teach Muslims to declare that Allah is the only God who is distinct from His creatures and to seek refuge only with Him. The *Al-Ikhlash*, for example, reads as follows:

> Say: He is Allah, the One;
>
> Allah the Eternal, Absolute;
>
> He begetteth not, Nor is He begotten;
>
> And there is none like unto Him.

This chapter of the Qur'an can be thought of as the primary message of Islam because of its role in reaffirming the *tauhid* of Allah (Bowen 1993:99–100).[14] And, indeed, Aa Gym recited this chapter, together with the following two chapters, to reaffirm his and his followers' belief in Allah as the only God in whom to believe and to whom worship is due.

Aa Gym's focus on *tauhid* can be seen further when the *wirid* continued

Hashbunallah	Sufficient unto us is Allah
wa ni'ma al-wakiel	He is the best Trustee
ni'ma al-maulaa wa ni'ma an-Nashier	The best Protector and the best Helper
Radhietu billahi rabba	I have chosen Allah as my only Lord
wa bi al-Islami diena	Islam as my religion
wa bi Muhammad an-nabiyya	Muhammad as my Prophet
wa rasuula	and messenger

Then Aa Gym chanted the commonly chanted phrases as follows:

Subhanallah [33 times]	Allah the Glorious
Alhamdulillah [33 times]	Praise be to Allah
Allohu Akbar [33 times]	Allah the Great

These three phrases are commonly chanted by Muslims 33 times after *shalat*. Aa Gym, however, seems to be more flexible in the number since he sometimes seems to chant the phrases less than 33 times. This suggests Aa Gym's inclination to follow his mood in doing optional rituals. [The *wirid* after *shalat* is not obligatory but optional in accord with all *madzhab* (schools of thought) in Islam.] After chanting these phrases 33 times, Aa Gym went on to utter

La ilaaha illallaahu wahdah,	There is no god but Allah Himself
la syariika lah,	He needs no partner
lahu al-mulku	To Him belongs the real kingdom

wa lahu al-hamdu	And to Him belong all praise
yuhyi wa yumiitu	It is He who gives life and death
wa hua 'ala qulli syai-in qadiir.	And He has power over all things
La haula wa laa quwwata	Neither power nor energy [all Creatures possess]
illaa bi allahi al-'aliyyi al-'adziim.	But given by Allah the High the Inaccessible
La ilaaha illa anta.	There is no god but You, O Allah
Subhaanaka	You are the Most Holy
innii kuntu min adz-dzalimiin.	I confess I am one of those who do wrong

The concentration on the *tauhid* is clearly seen in these phrases of *wirid*. Then, Aa Gym summoned the followers to say *sholawat* and each of the followers said

Allohumma sholli 'ala Muhammad	O Lord, bless the Prophet Muhammad
wa 'ala aali sayyidina Muhammad	And bless the family of the Prophet Muhammad

All these (sections of) *wirid* were uttered with an underlying tone of sadness. Aa Gym's voice during this *wirid* was a sad one, just like his voice during the *shalat* performance.

This version of *wirid* is just an example of a *wirid* performed at Daarut Tauhid after *shalat*. Aa Gym seems very flexible in this regard in that some parts of an utterance may sometimes not be uttered after *shalat*. The order is also flexible in respect of which phrase comes after which. Sometimes, during the *wirid*, Aa Gym inserts the following utterance of *istighfar*:

Astaghfirullaah al-'adziim [several times].

[I ask the forgiveness of Allah the Great.]

After the *wirid* is completed, Aa Gym then starts offering *do'a*. The *do'a* usually begins with a reflection focusing most often on death and sins. In other cases, the *do'a* and the reflection are done together, with the reflection in the middle of saying the *do'a*. Aa Gym himself, in offering the *do'a*, appears as though he is performing a self-reflection. He once told me that, in fact, when leading a communal *do'a*, "I simply talk to myself doing a sort of reflection on my life. I forswear and repent for my life's sins. I seek Allah's forgiveness for my mistakes and wrongs. I am, at the time, just trying to be aware of my sinful self as if I were offering the *do'a* on my own without any followers." Aa Gym then said that this was a way of doing something with *ikhlash* (sincerity) in that he did it without expectation of personal benefit from his followers.

The *do'a* offered on January 29, 1995, was begun by a reflection on death as follows.

O Allah, I know it will not be long before I die but I am not sure whether I am ready to face it. I know that I will soon be wrapped by a shroud, placed in *lubang lahat* [niche in the wall of a grave for the corpse], and be covered with dirt, but I am not ready enough. I definitely know that death is absolutely certain. I will no doubt be separated from my parents, although we do not know whether I or my parents will die first. Death will certainly separate me from my wife and children. Our love will, at a certain time, be stopped by death. When I die, people I leave behind might be sad or otherwise be "happy," laughing at my corpse.

I know You, O Allah, have told us that "Every soul shall have a taste of death [QS. 3:185]. I also know that *sakaratul maut* [mortal agony] is extremely painful. You, O Allah, give us the lesson of animals when being slaughtered. A sheep that is "sinless" shows, when being slaughtered, the painful state of its dying breath. A chicken, an animal that always makes *tashbih* [celebrating Allah's glory][15] and commits no sin, flaps when being slaughtered, demonstrating that dying is extremely painful. Given this lesson, I learn that my mortal agony will be much more painful that the animals' because I know I am sinful. Of course the more sinful one is, the more painful one's mortal agony will be.

O Allah, by death I will be leaving everything I love. I will be buried in the depth of the soil, accompanied by none and nothing but a shroud. It might even be my beloved relatives who heap the dirt over my corpse. I know that when dead I will leave behind all wealth, titles, degrees, status, and everything which often not only turns my attention away from You and make me derelict in *shalat, zakat*, and other obligations, but also force me sometimes to oppress others. This wealth I leave behind might even be spent by my offspring in ways of life beyond Your favour.

O Allah, on the Day of Judgement, You might address us: "*Hai dungu* [O you the foolish], how come you maltreated yourselves in the world. You never let your head bow in prostration. What preoccupied your mind was none other than worldly affairs, things that you have left behind without any use you could gain today. You often used your hands to oppress others whereas you never gave them a hand. Your eyes were sinful in looking at that which I had condemned looking upon while they were never used to read the Qur'an. Your ears were full of the sound of music and coarse language while they were never employed to listen attentively to religious truth. And, while you appeared to be always arrogant, why did you never lower your forehead to do a prostration on a *sajadah* (worship rug)?"

O Allah, it is very likely that at that time I will weep and wail, regretting my worldly life. A life which was full of sins and evils and lacked good

> deeds. I might also be punished earlier in the period of *barzakh* [16] because I know that punishment in the grave is certain. My body will be encased in the earth which hates a sinful corpse.

Aa Gym did this reflection firstly with a tone of sadness and later with crying and sobbing. The large number of followers, being completely involved in the reflection, followed Aa Gym as though they themselves said what Aa Gym was saying. They, who had been put into a sad state in the preceding *shalat*, cried easily as soon as Aa Gym began his reflective words. Tears trickled down their cheeks. Crying and sobbing could then be heard louder and louder as the reflection went on. While crying, many of the followers repeatedly called God by saying "O Allah, O Allah," or by mentioning God's Most Beautiful Names such as "O the Gracious, O the Powerful, O the Benefactor," etc. Some of them mumbled, saying, for instance, "Alas, I am unfortunate." Their behaviour, in short, showed total regret and repentance while at the same time hope for pardon and blessing from their God.

Then, when the followers had been made fully aware of their sinfulness, Aa Gym turned to offer the *do'a*, a request raised to Allah.

> O Allah, the only one who knows when we will die, remit all our sins and conceal all our mistakes. Please forgive our mistakes and errors, O the Most Indulgent. Pardon us, O God, for our ingratitude for all You have been giving. We truly apologise for our heedlessness in not helping those people badly in need.

> O Allah, the Most Indulgent the Merciful, please pardon our parents. Save them from Hell. Bless them with happiness and prosperity. Guide them in their last days of life, O Allah the Guide. Make it a happy ending and take their lives away in a *husnul khatimah* [17] state. Give them reward for their good deeds. Bless them with comfort in *barzakh*. Take the Hell out of their *kubur* [resting places], O the Most Hearer Being.

Here, when parents were dealt with by Aa Gym, the followers cried louder and many even wept. While weeping, some called their parents saying "O Daddy! O Mummy!" They were certainly reminded by Aa Gym's words of their mistakes and faithlessness toward their parents. In the meantime, Aa Gym just kept on offering the *do'a*, praying for other relatives as follows.

> O Lord, save all our brothers and sisters from a harmful life both here and hereafter. Guide them. Bring into the straight path those brothers and sisters who go astray. Bring harmony to our families here in the world. And keep it so next in Your Paradise.

> O Allah the Seer, please forgive the sins of our teachers, who have given us Your knowledge and guided us to the straight path. Pardon as well all people to whom we are indebted. Bless us with the capability to repay

the kindness of devout Muslims, Your servants. Please forgive the sins of anyone we ever hurt. And, similarly, please forgive other Muslims who ever hurt us.

O Allah the Very Loving, give us the ability to love and care so that we can love all Your beloved Muslims. At the same time, take away our oppressive characteristics so that we will not be cruelty against Your beloved Muslims.

O Allah who gives honour and strength, give us the best partner in life, a partner that You love and who loves You. Give men in attendance here the *shalihah* [virtuous] wives. Wives who will bring comfort to the family. Wives who are not lulled into and greedy for worldly pleasure. Wives who are worthy of being an example for the family and their descendants. Wives with beautiful character traits.

O Allah the Inaccessible, bless these Muslim women in attendance with the *shalih* (virtuous) husbands. Husbands who rely on and obey You. Husbands with the grace of benevolence, justice, and gentleness. Husbands who are willing to make a living that is *halal* (lawful) and *berkah* (fully blessed). Husbands who are worthy of being the pride and example for their family and descendants.

O Allah the Very Patient, bless with patience those Muslims to whom You have not yet given any partner for life. Empower them to look for one by the ways You favour.

O Allah the Dispenser of all good, entrust to us descendants who are *shalih* and *shalihah*. Allow our children to be good children who always pray to You for the welfare of their parents. Keep our children away from infidelity and indignity. Make their life in this world be useful and honourable. Make them leaders of devout Muslims who submit themselves to You.

Before finishing the *do'a*, Aa Gym may often give his followers some time to offer *do'a* individually for any request they want to make to Allah. They then prayed for their particular interests and Aa Gym prayed for himself. After some time, Aa Gym then raised his voice to continue leading the *do'a*.

O Allah who makes hearts fluctuate [muqallib al-qulub], let our minds be inclined to the truth. Make our hearts as hearts that are familiar with You, so that all we see in the world can make us learn more and more of Your majesty and glory. Make our minds always remember You, and our tongues always enjoy mentioning Your Beautiful Names. Make our ears love to listen to Your teachings. Make our hearts rely on and hope only for You. Let our hearts not fear other than You, not seek refuge other than You. Make our hearts love to remember You. Hearts that love You so much. Hearts that look forward to seeing You.

There is no god but You, O the Most Attentive. You are the only One whom we can rely on. Your care for Your Creation is ceaseless. Please accept our prayers, O our Lord. Verily, it is only You who can fulfil our hopes and prayers. *Amien*, O Allah the Cherisher and Sustainer of the Worlds.

Here the ritual *do'a* ended. The followers kept sitting for a while, reciting *al-Fatihah*, the first Chapter of the Qur'an, just like Muslims usually do after offering their prayers. Shortly afterwards, they shake hands with each others, many asking others' pardon for their personal mistakes if any. Many of the followers rush to approach Aa Gym to shake his hand or to embrace him. Nearly all kiss Aa Gym's hand, hoping for his *baraka* and asking him to pray to Allah for their behalf.

Aa Gym's representation in this *do'a* ritual and its preceding reflection is interesting. During the reflection Aa Gym represented himself by using the pronoun 'I' in saying the reflective words, as seen above, in offering the *do'a* he represented himself and the followers by using the pronoun 'we' instead of 'I'. This representation is important for two reasons. First, the followers are not offended although Aa Gym mentioned sins they had committed. Note that a person might be offended if one pointed out his or her sins because he or she might be ashamed. This is often the case in other sermons/talks at which a listener might be offended by the preacher's words. Second, by representing himself in the reflection, Aa Gym could recall all the sins of his past life and could hence experience to the fullest religious consciousness. In this way, the reflection can be done well.

5.5 Ritual Weeping: Meaning and Function

This tradition of spiritual weeping has to be understood as an inseparable part of the very nature of Pesantren Daarut Tauhid as the *Bengkel Akhlaq*. This can clearly be seen by understanding the meaning and function of the weeping.

First of all, the ritual weeping provides awareness of life's sins. Men and women involved in the Daarut Tauhid's activities and rituals come to the consciousness that their life has been full of mistakes and wrong doings in dealing with other people, this universe, and God. They realise that they have been causing ecological damage, destroying social relations, and neglecting Allah's commands for living in this world. They are, in short, awakened to the fact that they have been trapped in moral degradation. They express this consciousness in the form of tears.

Secondly, the ritual weeping offers *taubat*, in the sense of repentance. Men and women at Daarut Tauhid, being fully conscious of their sinfulness, regret their sinful life, particularly in the past. They humbly confess this before Allah in the ritual, by way of weeping.

Finally, the ritual weeping at Daarut Tauhid constitutes the manifest form of a high-standard of *taqwa* (piety). Pious Muslims are said to weep easily, not only because of sinfulness--although they rarely commit sins--but also because of the high quality of their faith. A santri said that "the ritual weeping, for them [devout Muslims] is the manifestation of faith [*iman*], that resides [*bersemayam*] in their heart, their sound heart, and their total submission to Allah, the Creator." Therefore the more pious one is the more frequently one would weep. A pious Muslim whose heart is sound may weep as often during spiritual contemplations and religious rituals as in daily life. In exemplifying this, another santri said that a pious Muslim may weep when viewing beautiful sights of this universe just because he is amazed by Allah's glory in creating those sights. Similarly, he or she may weep when witnessing environmental damage and social disorder engendered by Allah's creatures because he is "embarrassed" before Him. In any circumstance, a pious Muslim is said to be touched with the deepest emotion in his relation to Allah. This finds its outlet in tears.

Given these meanings, the ritual weeping at Daarut Tauhid have many important functions. First, the ritual weeping function as a means of personal purification. Crying here is an expression of *istighfar*, that is asking forgiveness from Allah, the Very Indulgent, for life's sins. "One might do *istighfar* without tears," a santri said, "but doing it with tears is an earnest request for Allah's pardon."

In its function as a means of personal purification, ritual weeping is also an expression of *taubat nasuha* (true repentance and forswearing). *Taubat* is a further step of *istighfar* and is deeper since *taubat* implies a promise for the future. By *taubat* one is both purifying oneself from any sins committed in the past and forswearing to Allah not to commit any sin in the future. Declaring *taubat* with tears is, to people at Daarut Tauhid, true repentance and earnest forswearing. The *taubat* is thus made more powerful by tears.

At first glance, the functions of ritual weeping may seem similar to children's crying which makes their request to their parent more likely to be attended to. In response to this impression, a santri said that what makes the *taubat* powerful is not the tears *per se* but the personal quality that generates the tears. The weeping, he explained, has to be generated from the depth of a perfect heart that holds true faith firmly. There is thus no point in pretending to cry in a ritual in order to draw Allah's attention as is the case with children-to-parent requests. Indeed, according to Ibn Qayyim Al-Jauziyah (cf. As-Sinjari 1994:54), ritual weeping is, for devout Muslims, a means by which to reach Paradise. Al-Jauziyah bases this on the Hadith of the Prophet Muhammad who said:

> No one sheds tears but Allah will save his body from the fire of Hell. If the tears trickle down a person's cheeks, his or her face will be saved from any degradation. If one out of a group of people cries, the whole group will be blessed by Allah. Only tears have unrestricted power. Verily, tears can extinguish the fire of Hell.

Using analogy, the Prophet Muhammad taught that the sincere tears of faithful Muslims can save them from Hell. It is this teaching of Islam that makes attractive and firm the tradition of ritual weeping at Daarut Tauhid.

Another function of ritual weeping is to intensify one's religiosity. Muslims at Daarut Tauhid believe that weeping can be viewed by Allah as a form of *amal shaleh* (good deed). This being so, weeping is thus rewarded by Allah. The more one weeps the more one is rewarded. The more one gains religious merits the more pious one, in turn, becomes. Ritual weeping can therefore make Muslims more and more devoutly religious.

The condition on this function of ritual weeping is that it has to be sincerely motivated by one's fear of Allah (As-Sinjari 1994:22-24, Azh-Zhahiry 1994:64-67). To fear Allah means to respect Him, obeying all His commands and avoiding all His prohibitions. In this regard, Muslims at Daarut Tauhid hold that tears would be in vain unless they otherwise reflect one's proper awe and respect of and one's loyalty and humility before Allah the Almighty (Azh-Zhahiry 1994:56). It is this kind of weeping that can effectively intensify one's religiosity.

Ritual weeping, with its all meanings and functions is of profound significance in increasing Daarut Tauhid's ability to attract followers. Indeed, weeping represents the very power of Daarut Tauhid to satisfy its followers. Daarut Tauhid's ability to make the followers weep is certainly a novel contribution to the development of Islam today, particularly among the youth.

ENDNOTES

[1] Daarut Tauhid's workshops for morality are thus more like church workshops and retreats for families and individuals, part of the Christian spiritual renewal that has flourished since the 1980s (Jensen 1989:94, 96).

[2] The word *hisab* evokes ideas of evaluating, counting, or measuring. *Hisab* in Islam is believed to be the "reckoning" that Allah will demand from all human beings on the Day of Judgement. Each will at the time be judged by way of accounting for their worldly actions. Those whose good deeds outnumber the bad will deserve paradise while the reverse will merit hell. This idea of rendering an account is actually comparable with that of Zoroastrian, Jewish, and Christian traditions.

[3] This view of Muslims at Daarut Tauhid on moral decadence is shared by many devout Muslims throughout Indonesia. For them, this decadence is symbolised by the Western life-style of nominal Muslims as observable through their provocative dress and their involvement in nightclub entertainment, pornographic film screenings, etc. (Kipp and Rodgers 1987:20; Muzaffar 1986:10-11).

[4] *Riya* denotes an intention to do something with the hope that others will *see* it and thus admire the doer. *Sum'ah* denotes actions performed in the hope that others will *hear* and thus praise the doer. Both connote the doer's arrogance. Whereas the outward actions which Islam requires must be done not only correctly but also with the correct intention, ie. not for fashion or to fit with a certain group. It must all be solely for the sake of Allah.

[5] As noted in many commentaries on the Qur'an, the word *qolbun* (heart), in Arabic understanding, is taken to be not only the seat of feelings and affections but also that of intelligence and resulting action. Heart thus implies the whole character, including what is meant by 'mind' in English.

[6] I have also noted in Chapter Two that this orientation towards *tauhid* was seen at the very beginning of Daarut Tauhid's development. Aa Gym's early gatherings, the embryo of Daarut Tauhid, were called *pengajian tauhid*.

[7] All the discussion about *ikhlash*, as understood by people at Daarut Tauhid, which is rooted in the Islamic scriptures, is just another datum that refutes Geertz's assertion that *ikhlash* is the core value of the *priyayi* group, which Geertz characterises to be influenced by the Hindu-Buddhist tradition. See Nakamura (1984:72) for further elaboration of this Geertzian error.

[8] Compare this to what Bowen (1993:296) found from the worshipping together among Muslims in Gayo. He suggests that worshipping together possibly brings to the fore one's relation to other people, produces aesthetical and emotional satisfaction, and embodies "certain ideas of religious communication and social relations."

[9] It happened that on the first Sunday of Ramadhan (February 5, 1995) Aa Gym was absent, fulfilling invitations for some religious talks in Singapore. The followers had not been advised of his absence in order to maintain the level of attendance. (The officials at Daarut Tauhid had learned from the drastic decrease in attendance during Aa Gym's absence for the *umrah* the month before.) Truly it worked effectively. The mosque was fully filled half an hour before time. The followers came in huge numbers, more than the usual number because it was the first of Ramadhan. (Ramadhan is the holy month to Muslims. They are more likely to attend religious activities during Ramadhan than in other months.) Certainly, those who attended the congregation were annoyed when they were told that the preacher for that Sunday would not be Aa Gym but Drs. H. Buchori Muslim, a prominent preacher in Bandung. Some in attendance expressed their disappointment when we were having a brief conversation. One of them argued that the current preacher was less attractive than Aa Gym, both in terms of the topic chosen and in the way it was delivered.

[10] The ground floor is used for the Daarut Tauhid's mini-market and is thus not part of the mosque.

[11] *Al-asma al-Husna* (the Most Beautiful Names) are the divine names of Allah. Muslims are taught by the Qur'an (7:179, for one) that to God belong the most Beautiful Names. A Hadith, transmitted by abu Hurairah, states: "to God belong 99 Names, a hundred less one; for He, the Odd Number likes (to be designated by these enumerated Names) one by one; whosoever knows the 99 Names will enter paradise." Muslims repeat these Names and meditate on them as an act of devotion. Chanting these names is known in the pesantren tradition as *dzikir istighothah*. And, according to the Sufi belief, remembering the names is a key to the secrets of life (Dhofier 1980a:183n).

[12] Chanting some verses of the Qur'an melodiously is a common part of Islamic ceremonial events in the Muslim tradition.

[13] QS. 49:13.

[14] Bowen shows the popularity of this chapter of the Qur'an among the Gayo people of Aceh. It is the first chapter that is memorised by heart by every Muslim born child. Like Bowen, Nakamura also notes the popularity of this chapter among Javanese for its beauty and strength (1984:72).

[15] It is taught in the Qur'an that all nature, including animals, sings the praises of Allah. Mountains, hills, creeping things, and flying fowl, together with prophets, angels, and men of God, are said to celebrate the glory of Allah (34:10, 38:18–19). Even the 'thunder repeateth His praises" (13:13). Thus whatever is in the heavens and the earth celebrates the praises of Allah (27:44, 57:1, 16:48–50).

[16] *Barzakh* is the place and time between death and the Last Judgement. The equivalent Indonesian term is *alam kubur* (lit. realm of the grave).

[17] *Husnul khatimah* literally means good ending. One is said to be *husnul khatimah* if one passed away at the time when one was fully pious. Technically, this state of *husnul khatimah* may be marked by one's utterance, in the very last second of life, of the *kalimah tauhid* (tauhid phrase) that is *la ilaha illallah* (there is no god but Allah).

Chapter 6: Conclusion

I have attempted to portray Pesantren Daarut Tauhid in terms of its emergence, its nature and structure, and the role it plays in the reinforcement of Islamic morality. The emergence of this pesantren in 1990 is part of the general resurgence of Islam in the world. It has been argued that the contemporary resurgence in Muslim societies, particularly in urban areas, can be understood as the continuation of the spirit of reformist renewal in Islam. Christian Kiem (1993:92), observing Muslim youth in Eastern Indonesia, argues that Islamic resurgence among the youth in Muslim countries has to be understood as "an intra-Islamic...purification of religious life from pre-Islamic beliefs and practices." In a similar tone, Rifqi Rosyad (1995:115) argues that the Islamic resurgence among the Muslim youth in Bandung..."is a continuation of *tajdid* (renewal) tradition in Muslim societies." Seen in this way, the resurgence is most often linked to the reformist movements that undermine the position of Islamic traditionalists. Kiem evidently links the resurgence in Ternate to Muhammadiyah and Rosyad links the resurgence in Bandung to Muhammadiyah and Persis. Both Muhammadiyah and Persis represent the modernist, reformist line of Islamic thought.

Such an argument is not always an accurate representation of the diversity and complexity which is the very nature of Islamic resurgence throughout the Muslim world (Dessouki 1982:6). While the internal purification from traditional practices of Islam may be the chief aim of some cases of Islamic resurgence, it is not the aim of many others. I see an inclination among Muslim youth to leave behind the exhausting conflict between modernist-traditionalist groups. This results in a decreasing concern with questioning one's practice of Islam. The question whether or not one's practice of Islam is "Islamic,"--viewed from modernist point of view, anyway--is now less important than whether or not one practises Islam at all. Hence I argue that associating the resurgence with theological reformism is less relevant than previously.

In support of this, Dhofier (1980a:342-3) has shown the inadequacy of this approach based on a traditionalist-modernist dichotomy. Lessons from Pesantren Daarut Tauhid demonstrate that Muslims are less concerned with the different views and practices of the modernist and traditionalist groups. Their primary concern is that, to cope with pervading social ills, Muslims have to practise their Islam, regardless of whose group of Islamic practices they follow. Thus Muslim youth at Daarut Tauhid put emphasis on *akhlaq* (Islamic morality), an aspect of Islamic teaching that is conceived of in the same way by both modernist and traditionalist groups and so does not cause a split. What has divided Muslim societies into modernist and traditionalist groups has mainly been *fiqh* (Islamic jurisprudence), for there are many *ikhtilaf* (different views) in Islamic thought in this regard. I therefore argue that Muslims at Daarut Tauhid are neither modernist nor traditionalist but a combination of the two.

This combination is clear from the Islam that is practised at Daarut Tauhid. Modernist traditions in Pesantren Daarut Tauhid can be seen in two respects. First, Pesantren Daarut Tauhid applies some modernist practices for Islamic rites. For example, it practises the modernist style of eight cycles *shalat tarawih* in Ramadhan. Second, it tangibly attempts to adopt modern technology, if Kiem (1993:104) is justifiable in his assumption that the modernists are more open to adopt Western technology than the traditionalists.

Traditionalist practices in Daarut Tauhid are also clear. In fact, being a pesantren, Daarut Tauhid bears more traditionalist features. This is because the pesantren tradition itself is identified with the traditional line of Islamic thought, regardless of the fact that a reformist kind of "pesantren" is now developing. Thus, Daarut Tauhid has many features in common with the pesantren tradition in general.

Pesantren Daarut Tauhid, as we have seen, grew out of a small *pengajian*, just like other pesantren (Dhofier 1980a; 1982). But, unlike the common case that a pesantren is established by a learned pesantren graduate or by a hereditary *kyai* (Dhofier 1980a:72-73; Horikoshi 1976:186-191), Daarut Tauhid was founded by a young leader born to an army-family and a graduate from an academy of technology. Thus, to be a religious specialist, Aa Gym lacked both genealogical legitimacy and intellectual competence. To overcome these deficiencies some rites were extremely crucial to the *kyai*ship of Aa Gym. These were the *i'tikaf* and the *hajj*. The *i'tikaf* Aa Gym carried out during Ramadhan in 1987 and the *hajj* he performed two months later transformed his personality and the perception of people about him. The *i'tikaf* and the *hajj* functioned as a phase of liminality, in that Aa Gym stayed "at a distance" from people and reflected on his personality and spirituality. After the *i'tikaf* and the *hajj* were completed, Aa Gym began to qualify as a religious leader. This was supported by several dreams that revealed the future leadership of Aa Gym. Therefore, the *i'tikaf*, the *hajj*, and the dreams were sources of legitimacy to Aa Gym's *kyai*ship.

Seen from the perspective of the founder, the case of Daarut Tauhid is like the case of Pesantren Tegal Rejo, which was founded by a *priyayi* (Pranowo 1991). Further, as in the case of Daarut Tauhid, Pranowo has also noted a certain degree of creative expression of Islam pioneered by Pesantren Tegal Rejo. The difference lies more in terms of their 'target' of creativity: while Tegal Rejo creatively employed local culture, Daarut Tauhid creatively modifies a more global culture than the local one. The reason for this is certainly the location: Tegal Rejo is rural whereas Daarut Tauhid is urban. Thus, the challenge is different but the response to it is similar, in that both tend to incorporate, rather than to oppose, the challenge, with necessary modification.

Unlike Horikoshi (1976), I argue that the relationship between Aa Gym, the *kyai*, and his followers is both collective and personal. Horikoshi, studying the *kyai* in West Java, argues that the *kyai* "must maintain a certain distance from the masses to preserve the image of a symbolic leader not easily accessible to the public." (1976:368) As we have seen, Aa Gym develops an intimate sphere of interaction with his followers. The religious advice and consultations at Daarut Tauhid are not impersonal in nature. Yet, Aa Gym, like other *kyai*, remains charismatic in the eyes of his followers. This may follow the leader-follower relationship in Javanese tradition, which is, as Murtono pointed out, "a personal and close tie of mutual respect and responsibility" (cf. Guinness 1986:180). Hence, I argue that the *kyai* leadership, like the leadership among Ledok people in Yogyakarta (Guinness 1986:181), is conceived of less as a privilege than as a religious responsibility. The *kyai* is offered trust on the basis of his community mindedness and less on the basis of his personal following.

In the reinforcement of Islamic morality, Pesantren Daarut Tauhid has made a contribution to the pesantren tradition at large. It is true that the intention of all pesantren is to refine the morality of their students, educate their spirits, propagate virtue, teach propriety, and prepare them for a life of sincerity and purity (Dhofier 1980a:10). However, at other pesantren, this embedment of morality is confined to the *santri* who stay at the pesantren complex. These *santri* are in turn supposed to be the living examples of Islamic morality when they return home. Thus, generally speaking, the role of the pesantren in the application of Islamic morality among Muslim community is indirect, that is, the *kyai* and the *santri* become examples of correct Islamic behaviour (Dhofier 1980a:6; 1982:19).

By contrast, the role Pesantren Daarut Tauhid plays in the reinforcement of Islamic morality is quite direct. This is clearly seen through several factors. First, its popular name, Pesantren *Bengkel Akhlaq*, reflects its deliberate focus on reinforcing morality in the Muslim community. Second, the life of the pesantren is also developed in a moral minded sphere, in terms of oral and bodily behaviour. Third, Islamic morality is always the central theme of the public sermons and the written publications issued by the pesantren. Fourth, the main activity is spiritual workshops which aim at rehabilitating the morality of the Muslim community. In fact, the idea of these workshops originated from the short course tradition common to nearly all pesantren. In West Java, it is known as *pasaran*, that is, a short course in Ramadhan during which one or two *kitab* (Islamic texts), usually thick enough, are marathonly read to the end. More recently, this tradition is called *pesantren kilat*, held commonly in Ramadhan in many pesantren and mosques. Nonetheless, the *pasaran* and the *pesantren kilat* is generally concerned more with the mastering of Islamic knowledge than with the practical application of Islamic morality in daily life. This latter is more the concern of

Pesantren Daarut Tauhid. I argue that it is for this form of moral workshop that Pesantren Daarut Tauhid draws the attention of Muslim youth in urban Bandung.

The reinforcement of Islamic morality at Daarut Tauhid is made more effective by the creation of the tradition of ritual weeping. Daarut Tauhid established an individual and communal tradition of ritual weeping. This constitutes a novel feature of the pesantren tradition in Java. There may have already existed a tradition of spiritual weeping among Muslims, mostly among Sufi. However, it is individual in nature and as a result is not socially recognised. By means of this weeping, Muslims at Daarut Tauhid effectively control their life: becoming religiously conscious, they purify themselves from any sin and immorality and pursue the highest standard of piety and righteousness. Tears mean, to them, fear and obedience, submission and relief.

It is by way of reinforcing this Islamic morality that Islam in Bandung is "gaining energy" among Muslim youth. To gain this energy, Islam does not have to lose its definition, as Geertz suggests it has (1995:165). If Geertz bases his judgment on his observation that the ills of modern life are taking shape among Muslims (1995:142-143), Daarut Tauhid might be used to counter Geertz's proposition. Daarut Tauhid attempts to reinforce Islamic morality and, as a result, it gains energy. Thus, to gain energy, Muslims have to confirm, and not to abandon, the definition of Islam. Certainly, lessons from the case of Pesantren Daarut Tauhid demonstrate that Islam, in Indonesia and elsewhere, is now gaining energy by maintaining the definition of Islam.

Selected Glossary

A

Aa	Sundanese term to address young, respected person
Adzan	call to summon to *shalat* (prayer)
Ahli ibadah	totally devout
Ajengan	Islamic teachers among the Sundanese
Ajudan	guardian, servant
Akhlaq	morality, morals
al-Asma al-Husna	the most beautiful names (of God)
Alhamdulillah	praise be to Allah
Amal	deeds, performances of religious rituals and social obligations
Amal shaleh	good deeds
Aurat	parts of body which have to be covered

B

Baitullah	the house of Allah/mosque
Barakah	divine blessing
Batin	esoteric, inner, inward
Beca	pedicab
Bedug	large drum to summon to *shalat* (prayer)
Bengkel Akhlaq	Workshop of Morality
Bening	clear, pure

C

Ceramah	speech, talk

D

Daarut Tauhid	hamlet of the Oneness of God

Dakwah	Muslim missionary activity/proselytization
Do'a	invocation/prayer for a blessing from God
Dzikir	remembrance of God (commonly by recollecting God's names or certain phrases by which to praise God)
Dzikir khafi	*dzikir* in a very low tone
Dzikir zahar	loud *dzikir*

F

Faqih	expert on *fiqh*, religious scholar
Fiqh	Islamic jurisprudence

G

Ghibah	gossip

H

Hadith	traditions purporting to preserve the decisions, actions, and utterances of the Prophet Muhammad.
Haji	pilgrim (title for Muslims who have performed pilgrimage to Mecca)
Hajj	pilgrimage to Mecca (obligatory, once in life)
Halal	lawful, religiously allowed
Haram	religiously forbidden
Hati	heart, mind
Hikmah	divine wisdom, lesson
Hisab	accountability

I

I'tikaf	retreat/stay in a mosque
Ibadah	worship/act of pure devotion
Iblis	Satan, devil

Ikhlas/iklas	sincerity, to obey God sincerely and only for His pleasure
Ikhtiar	endeavour, attempt, effort
IKIP	*Institut Keguruan Ilmu Pengetahuan* (Teachers' Training College)
Ilapat	divine inspiration, foretell, foresee
Ilham	personal inspiration
Ilmu ladunni	God-given knowledge (knowledge that is not learned but is granted by God).
Imam	head of communal *shalat* (prayer)
Iman	faith
Irhash	miraculous acts granted by God to prophets before their prophethood
Iri-dengki	envy, jealousy
Istidraj	miraculous acts given by God to non-Muslims, just to spoil them.
Istigfar	requesting Allah's pardon
Istiqomah	consistency
ITB	*Institut Teknologi Bandung* (Bandung Institute of Technology)

J

Jemaah	followers
Jenderal	general
Jujur/kejujuran	honesty

K

Karamah (kramat)	miraculous gifts granted by God to Islamic saints
Karyawan	workers, clerks
Keridoan	God's favour and pleasure
Kerudung	female head cover (also known as *jilbab*)
Keselamatan	salvation

Ketenangan batin	inner peace, inner easiness
Khusnul khatimah	happy ending, virtuous ending of life
Komandan	commander
Kopeah	cap
Kultus individu	the cult of the individual
Kurnia	blessing
Kyai	a title for Islamic scholars who generally lead a pesantren

L

Lahat	niche in the wall of grave for the corpse
Lahir	exoteric, outer, outward
Lailatul Qodar	the night of power/determinism
Lintas alam	cross-country

M

Ma'rifatullah	gnosis, to know Allah
Ma'unah	miraculous acts granted by God to *ulama* and pious Muslims
Maksiat	wickedness, immoral conduct
Managemen Allah	divine management
Mandi taubat	bath of repentance
Masantren	live in pesantren
Maslahat	prosperity/benefit
Mazhab	school of thought
Menwa	*Resimen Mahasiswa* (University Student Regiment, Military training for University students)
Mu'jizat	Miraculous attributes granted by God to all Prophets
Muballigh	Islamic preacher
Muhasabah	introspection

Mukhlisin	sincere people
Munkarot	disavowals
Murid	student in Sufi orders
Mursyid	guides, teachers in Sufi orders

N

Nasabah	customers
Niat	intention

O

Opsih	*operasi bersih* (clean-up activities)

P

Pengajian	public sermon/religious talk/learning group
Pesantren	Islamic cultural institution/Islamic Boarding school
Pondok	dormitory (it may also mean pesantren)

Q

Qolbun salim	sound heart, sound mind

R

Rihlah	tour, excursion
Riya	show-off, doing things just for fashion
Riyadhoh	exercise, training
Ru'ya shadiqah	true visions

S

Sabar	patience
Sakaratul maut	mortal agony

Santri	student of pesantren/pious Muslim
Sejuk hati	inner comfort
Shalat	the prescribed form of prayer in Islam
Shalawat	invocation (requesting God's blessing for the Prophet)
Shalih	pious man
Shalihah	pious woman
Shaum	fasting
Shilaturrahmi	bonds of friendship
Shodaqoh	charity
Sipenmaru	*Seleksi Penerimaan Mahasiswa Baru* (Entry Selection for University Student)
Slamet	in peace, saved
SMA	*Sekolah Menengah Atas* (Upper High School)
SMP	*Sekolah Menengah Pertama* (Lower High School)
Subhanallah	Glory be to Allah/ Allah the Most Holy
Sujud	prostration
Sum'ah	show-off

T

Tadarrus	recitation of the Qur'an
Tahajjud	optional midnight *shalat*
Takabbur	haughty, arrogance
Taubat	repenting and forswearing
Tauhid	the oneness of God
Taushiyah	religious advice
Taushiyah Penyejuk Hati	Comforting Religious Advice
Tawaddu	modesty, humility
Tawekal	trust in God
Terjun payung	parachute jumping

U

Ukhuwwah Islamiyah	Islamic brotherhood
Ulama	Islamic scholars
Ummat	Islamic community
Umrah	lesser, optional pilgrimage to Mecca
Unisba	*Universitas Islam Bandung* (Bandung Islamic University)
Unpad	*Universitas Pajajaran* (Pajajaran University)

W

Wali	Muslim saint
Wartel	*warung telkom* (telecom shop)
Wirid	routine programme of dzikir

Z

Zakat	religious alms
Zuhud	asceticism

Bibliography

Ahmad, Khurshid. 1983. "The Nature of Islamic Resurgence" in *Voices of Resurgent Islam*. J. L. Esposito (ed.), pp. 218–229. New York: Oxford University Press.

Amstrong, Karen. 1991. *Muhammad: a Western Attempt to Understand Islam*. London: Victor Gollancz Ltd.

As-Sinjari, A. 1994. "Mengapa Takut pada Allah" in *Menangis karena Takut pada Allah*. Trans. by Farid Ma'ruf and Kathur Suhardi. Pp. 16–47. Jakarta: Pustaka Al Kautsar.

As-Suhaibany, A. A. 1994. "Sosok Orang-orang Suka Menangis dan Takut kepada Allah dari Kalangan Sahabat" in *Menangis karena Takut pada Allah*. Trans. by Farid Ma'ruf and Kathur Suhardi. Pp. 74–92. Jakarta: Pustaka Al-Kautsar.

Atjeh, H. Abubakar. 1957. *Sejarah Hidup K.H.A. Wahid Hasjim dan Karangan Tersiar*. Jakarta: Panitia Buku Peringatan Alm. K. H. A. Wahid Hasjim.

Azh-Zhahiry, A. A. 1994. "Menangis dan Takut kepada Allah" in *Menangis karena Takut pada Allah*. Trans. by Farid Ma'ruf and Kathur Suhardi. Pp. 48–73. Jakarta: Pustaka Al Kautsar.

Bachtiar, H. W. 1985. "The Religion of Java: A Commentary" in *Readings on Islam in Southeast Asia*. A. Ibrahim et al (eds.), pp. 278–285. Singapore: Institute of Southeast Asian Studies.

Bailey, D. J. 1986. *Rural Islam in Sundanese Java: A Cultural Interpretation of Peasant Resistance*. Ph.D thesis, Department of Anthropology, University of Sydney.

Bell, C. 1992. *Ritual Theory Ritual Practice*. Oxford: Oxford University Press.

Bowen, J. R. 1987. "Islamic Transformations: From Sufi Doctrine to Ritual Practice in Gayo Culture" in *Indonesian Religions in Transition*. R. S. Kipp and S. Rodgers (eds.), pp. 113–135. Tucson: The University of Arizona Press.

Bowen, J. R. 1993. *Muslims Through Discourse: Religion and Ritual in Gayo Society*. Princeton: Princeton University Press.

Cantory, L. J. 1990. "The Islamic Revival as Conservatism and as Progress in Contemporary Egypt" in *Religious Resurgence and Politics in the Contemporary World*. E. Sahliyeh (ed.). New York: State University of New York Press.

Dessouki, A. E. H. 1982. *Islamic Resurgence in the Arab World*. New York: Praeger.

Dewey, A. G. 1962. *Peasant Marketing in Java*. New York: The Free Press of Glencoe Inc.

Dhofier, Zamakhsyari. 1980a. *The Pesantren Tradition: A Study of the Role of the Kyai in the Maintenance of the Traditional Ideology of Islam in Java*. Ph.D Thesis, The Australian National University, Canberra.

Dhofier, Zamakhsyari. 1980b. "Islamic Education and Traditional Ideology on Java" in *Indonesia: the Making of a Culture*. J. J. Fox (ed.), pp. 263–271. Canberra: Research School of Pacific Studies.

Dhofier, Zamakhsyari. 1980c. "Kinship and Marriage among the Javanese Kyai" in *Indonesia* No. 29: pp. 47–58.

Dhofier, Zamakhsyari. 1982. *Tradisi Pesantren: Studi Tentang Pandangan Hidup Kyai*. Jakarta: LP3ES.

Dhofier, Zamakhsyari. 1984. "Relevansi Pesantren dan Pengembangan Ilmu di Masa Depan" in *Pesantren*. No. Perdana: 20–25.

Eaton, H. Gai. 1994. "Reflections on Two Travel Books: Dessert Encounter and the Hadj." *The Islamic Quarterly*. Vol. XXXVIII (4):283–291.

Esposito, J. L. (ed.) 1983. *Voices of Resurgent Islam*. New York: Oxford University Press.

Fluehr-Lobban, Carolyn. 1994. *Islamic Society in Practice*. Florida: The University of Florida Press.

Fox, J. J. 1991. "Ziarah Visits to the Tombs of the Wali, The Founder of Islam on Java" in *Islam in the Indonesian Social Context*. M. C. Ricklefs (ed.), pp. 19–38. Clayton: Centre of Southeast Asian Studies, Monash University.

Geertz, Clifford. 1960. "The Javanese Kyai: The Changing Role of A Cultural Broker" in *Comparative Study in Society and History*. Vol. II. Pp. 228–249.

Geertz, Clifford. 1969. "Modernisation in a Muslim Society: The Indonesian Case" in *Man, State, and Society in Contemporary Southeast Asia*. Robert O. Tilman (ed.), pp. 201–211. New York: Praeger Publishers.

Geertz, Clifford. 1976. *The Religion of Java*. Chicago: The University of Chicago Press.

Geertz, Clifford. 1979. "'Internal Conversion' in Contemporary Bali" in *Reader in Comparative Religion: An Anthropological Approach*. Fourth Edition. William A. Lessa and Evon. Z. Vogt (eds.), pp. 444–454. New York: Harper Collins Publishers.

Geertz, Clifford. 1993. *The Interpretation of Cultures*. London: Fontana Press.

Geertz, Clifford. 1995. *After the Fact: Two Countries, Four Decades, One Anthropologist*. Cambridge: Harvard University Press.

Gibb, H. A. R. and J. H. Kramers (eds.). 1961. *Shorter Encyclopaedia of Islam*. Leiden: E. J. Brill.

Glicken, J. 1987. "Sundanese Islam and the Value of *Hormat*: Control, Obedience, and Social Location in West Java" in *Indonesian Religions in Transition*. R. S. Kipp and S. Rodgers (eds.), pp. 238–252. Tucson: The University of Arizona Press.

Guinness, Patrick. 1986. *Harmony and Hierarchy in A Javanese Kampung*. Singapore: Oxford University Press.

Guinness, Patrick. 1994. "Local Society and Culture" in *Indonesia's New Order: The Dynamics of Socio-economic Transformation*. Hal Hill (ed.), pp. 267–304. Sydney: Allen & Unwin.

Hefner, R. W. 1993. "Of Faith and Commitment: Christian Conversion in Muslim Java" in *Conversion to Christianity: Historical and Anthropological Perspectives on a Great Transformation*. R. W. Hefner (ed.), pp. 99–125. Berkeley: University of California Press.

Hill, Brennan R. 1988. *Key Dimensions of Religious Education*. Minnesota: Saint Mary's Press.

Hodgson, M. G. S. 1974. *The Venture of Islam: Conscience and History in a World Civilisation*. Vol. 2 (The Expansion of Islam in the Middle Periods). Chicago: The University Of Chicago Press.

Horikoshi, H. 1976. *A Traditional Leader in a Time of Change: The Kyai and Ulama in West Java*. Ann Arbour: University Microfilm International.

Horikoshi, H. 1980. "*Asrama*: An Islamic Psychiatric Institution in West Java." *Social Sciences and Medicine*. Vol. 14B, pp. 157–165.

Jamhari. 1994. "Indonesia Dalam Imaginasi Geertz." Paper presented in a seminar on *Kritik dan Apresiasi terhadap Indonesianists*, August 13, 1994, Indonesian Embassy, Canberra.

Jamhari. 1995. *To Visit A Sacred Tomb: The Practice of Ziarah to Sunan Tembayad's Resting Place in Klaten, Java*. MA thesis, Department of Archaeology and Anthropology, The Australian National University, Canberra.

Jensen, I. K. Khin. 1989. "Belief in God: Impetus for Social Action" in *Social Consequences of Religious Belief*. William Reace Garrett (ed.), pp. 91–99. New York: Paragon House.

Johns, Anthony H. 1975. "Islam in Southeast Asia: Reflections and New Directions" in *Indonesia*. No. 19:33–55.

Karim, I. A. 1993. *Kegiatan Dakwah 'Daarut Tauhid' dan Pengaruhnya terhadap Perilaku Para Remaja*. Skripsi, Department of Dakwah, State Institute for Islamic Studies, Bandung.

Karim, M. Rusli. 1995. "Agama dan Keadilan Sosial." *Republika*. November 17, 1995.

Kiem, Christian. 1993. "Re-Islamization among Muslim Youth in Ternate Town, Eastern Indonesia" in *Sojourn* 8 (1): 92–127.

Kipp, R. S. and S. Rodgers. 1987. "Introduction: Indonesian Religions in Society" in *Indonesian Religions in Transition*. R. S. Kipp and S. Rodgers (eds.), pp. 1–31. Tucson: The University of Arizona Press.

Koentjaraningrat, R. M. 1963. "Book Review: Clifford Geertz, The Religion of Java" in *Majalah Ilmu-ilmu Sastra Indonesia*. No. 1.

Koentjaraningrat, R. M. 1984. *Kebudayaan Jawa*. Jakarta: P. N. Balai Pustaka.

Madjid, N. 1988. "Pesantren dan Tasauf" in *Pesantren dan Pembaharuan*. 4th edition. M. D. Raharjo (ed.), pp. 94–120. Jakarta: LP3ES.

Mastuhu. 1990. "Gaya dan Suksesi Kepemimpinan Pesantren" in *Ulumul Qur'an* No. 7 Vol. III: pp. 88–97.

Mastuhu. 1994. *Dinamika Sistem Pendidikan Pesantren: Satu Kajian Tentang Unsur dan Nilai Sistem Pendidikan Pesantren*. Jakarta: Indonesian-Nederlands Cooperation in Islamic Studies (INIS).

Morris, Brian. 1987. *Anthropological Studies of Religion: An Introductory Text*. Cambridge: Cambridge University Press.

Muchtarom, Z. 1988. *Santri dan Abangan di Jawa*. Jakarta: Indonesian-Nederlands Cooperation in Islamic Studies (INIS).

Munawar-Rachman, B. and Asep Usman Ismail. 1991. "Cinta Tuhan di Tempat Matahari Terbit: Tarekat Qadiriyah-Naqsyabandiyah di Suryalaya." *Ulumul Qur'an* No. 8 Vol. II:100–105.

Muzaffar, C. 1986. "Islamic Resurgence: A Global View (with Illustrations from Southeast Asia)" in *Islam and Society in Southeast Asia*. T. Abdullah and S. Siddique (eds.). Singapore: Institute of Southeast Asian Studies.

Muzaffar, C. 1987. *Islamic Resurgence in Malaysia*. Petaling Jaya: Penerbit Fajar Bakti.

Nakamura, M. 1983. *The Crescent Arises over the Banyan Tree: A Study of the Muhammadiyah Movement in A Central Javanese Town*. Yogyakarta: Gadjah Mada University Press.

Nakamura, M. 1984. "The Cultural and Religious Identity of Javanese Muslims: Problems of Conceptualisation and Approach." *Prisma* No. 31.

Nurol-Aen, I. 1990. "Inabah" in *Thoriqot Qodiriyyah Naqsyabandiyyah: Sejarah, Asal-usul, dan Perkembangannya*. Harun Nasution (ed.), pp. 391–420. Tasikmalaya: Institut Agama Islam Latifah Mubarokiyyah.

Pemberton, J. 1994. *On the Subject of "Java."* Ithaca: Cornell University Press.

Pranowo, M. B. 1991a. *Creating Islamic Tradition in Rural Java*. Ph.D Thesis. Department of Anthropology and Sociology, Monash University, Melbourne.

Pranowo, M. B. 1991b. "Traditional Islam in Contemporary Rural Java" in *Islam in the Indonesian Social Context*. M. C. Ricklefs (ed.), pp. 39–54. Clayton: Centre of Southeast Asian Studies, Monash University.

Prasojo, S. et.al. 1974. *Profil Pesantren: Laporan Hasil Penelitian Pesantren Al-Falak dan Delapan Pesantren Lain di Bogor*. Jakarta: LP3ES.

Raharjo, M. D. 1975. "The Kyai, the Pesantren, and the Village: A Preliminary Sketch." *Prisma* 1:32–43.

Raharjo, M. D. 1982. "Kehidupan Pemuda Santri: Penglihatan dari Jendela Pesantren di Pabelan" in *Pemuda dan Perubahan Sosial*. Taufik Abdullah (ed.), pp. 90–112. Jakarta: LP3ES.

Raharjo, M. D. 1988. "Dunia Pesantren dalam Peta Pembaharuan" in *Pesantren dan Pembaharuan*. 4th edition. M. D. Raharjo (ed.), pp. 1–38. Jakarta: LP3ES.

Raillon, F. 1985. *Politik dan Ideologi Mahasiswa Indonesia: Pembentukan dan Konsolidasi Orde Baru 1966–1974*. Jakarta: LP3ES.

Ricklefs, M. C. 1991. *Islam in the Indonesian Social Context*. Clayton: Centre of Southeast Asian Studies, Monash University.

Rosyad, R. 1995. *A Quest for True Islam: A Study of the Islamic Resurgence Movement among the Youth in Bandung, Indonesia*. MA thesis. Department of Archaeology and Anthropology, the Australian National University, Canberra.

Seymour-Smith, C. 1986. *Macmillan Dictionary of Anthropology*. London: The Macmillan Press Ltd.

Steenbrink, K. A. 1986. *Pesantren, Madrasah, Sekolah: Pendidikan Islam dalam Kurun Modern*. Jakarta: LP3ES.

Su'dan, R. H. 1991. "Penyembuhan Penderita Kecanduan Narkotika di Pesantren Suryalaya" in *Pesantren Sebagai Wadah Komunikasi*. Sindu Galba, pp. 73–80. Jakarta: Proyek Inventarisasi Nilai-nilai Budaya, Departemen Pendidikan dan Kebudayaan.

Tebba, S. 1985. "Dilemma Pesantren: Belenggu Politik dan Pembaruan Sosial" in *Pergulatan Dunia Pesantren: Membangun dari Bawah*. M. Dawam Raharjo (ed.), pp. 267–288. Jakarta: Perhimpunan Pengembangan Pesantren dan Masyarakat.

The Kingdom of Saudi Arabia. 1993. *The Qur'an; English Translation of "The Meanings and Commentary."* Medina: King Fahd Complex for the Printing of the Holy Qur'an.

Trimingham, J. S. 1971. *The Sufi Orders in Islam*. Oxford: Oxford University Press.

Van Bruinessen, M. 1992. "Pesantren dan Kitab Kuning: Pemeliharaan dan Kesinambungan Tradisi Pesantren" in *Ulumul Qur'an* No. 4 Vol. III: 73–85.

Wahid, A. 1984. "Asal-usul Tradisi Keilmuan di Pesantren." *Pesantren*. No. 1:4–11.

Woodward, M. R. 1989. *Islam in Java: Normative Piety and Mysticism in the Sultanate of Yogyakarta*. Tuscon: The University of Arizona Press.

Zulkifli. 1994. *Sufism in Java: The Role of the Pesantren in the Maintenance of Sufism in Java*. MA thesis, Department of Archaeology and Anthropology, The Australian National University, Canberra.

www.ingramcontent.com/pod-product-compliance
Lightning Source LLC
Chambersburg PA
CBHW060947170426
43197CB00031B/2988